"Paula Munier's *Writing with Quiet Hands* is the real deal. Munier knows writing and publishing from all the angles and covers them in such a way as to teach, inspire, and encourage. If you want to learn, turn the pages and behold." —Reed Farrel Coleman *New York Times* best-selling author of Robert B. Parker's *The Devil Wins*

"Paula Munier has been a wizard behind the scenes of the New England mystery community for years. In *Writing with Quiet Hands*, she makes her wisdom available to everyone who's ever thought about writing a novel. It's a practical, inspiring handbook on the craft and practice of writing, and the next best thing to taking one of her workshops." —Joseph Finder, *New York Times* best-selling author of *The Fixer* and *Suspicion*

"*Writing with Quiet Hands* is loaded with tips and tools, firsthand experience, and down-to-earth advice from a writer, editor, and agent who's seen it from all sides. Paula Munier gives it to you straight as she dissects the inspiration, perspiration, and dogged determination it takes to set and meet your writing goals. This book will keep you sane." —Hallie Ephron, *New York Times* best-selling author of *Night Night, Sleep Tight*

"In the tradition of Stephen King's *On Writing*, Paula Munier embeds her sound advice on every aspect of writing—from drafts to rewrites to getting published—into her own inspirational story of her life as an editor, author, and agent. Blending personal anecdotes, examples from published authors, and prompts for the aspiring writer, *Writing with Quiet Hands* is a well-rounded guide that deserves a place on every writer's bookshelf." —Kim van Alkemade, author of *Orphan #8*

writing with quiet hands

how to shape your writing to resonate with readers

paula munier

WRITER'S DIGEST
BOOKS

WritersDigest.*com*
Cincinnati, Ohio

For more resources for writers, visit www.writersdigest.com.

19 18 17 16 15   5 4 3 2 1

Distributed in Canada by Fraser Direct
100 Armstrong Avenue
Georgetown, Ontario, Canada L7G 5S4
Tel: (905) 877-4411

Distributed in the U.K. and Europe by F+W Media International
Brunel House, Newton Abbot, Devon, TQ12 4PU, England
Tel: (+44) 1626-323200, Fax: (+44) 1626-323319
E-mail: postmaster@davidandcharles.co.uk

Distributed in Australia by Capricorn Link
P.O. Box 704, Windsor, NSW 2756 Australia
Tel: (02) 4577-3555

ISBN13: 978-1-59963-923-9

Edited by Rachel Randall
Designed by Alexis Brown
Production coordinated by Debbie Thomas

dedication
For Michael,
because in life, as in a good story,
we can never really know
what's going to happen next.

table of contents

foreword

It's one of those memories we all can share, if we're lucky. We're little kids, and we say to someone who loves us—or who is trying to get us to go to sleep—"Tell me a story." And if we're lucky, that person who loves us puts us on their lap, or sits on the bed beside us, and begins to weave a tale. "Once upon a time ..." they say, and our real world falls away. No more walls, no more bedroom, no more reality. We enter the world of the story, delighted to go through that reliable and recognizable portal of promise, the magical words "Once upon a time."

But Grandma or Aunt Sally or Sister Susie hadn't studied storytelling, or been awarded an MFA, or become a best-selling author. They simply and quietly understood what a story needs: a character, a setting, a problem, a quest, a happy (for some) ending. And as young listeners, we knew what to expect. *Here comes the exciting part*, we'd think. *Here comes the scary part.* Even though the storyteller was making it up on the spot.

Because even back then, we knew about stories. The rhythm and poetry and music and life and passion of stories is hard-wired, I'm sure of it.

Time passed, as it always does, and the roads diverged in the yellow woods. And for some of us, the listener became the storyteller. But somehow, instead of joyfully creating a story from experience and imagination, we made it difficult. *I'm a writer now*, we think. *And this had better be good. It has to be good! How do I make it Good? How do I sell it? How do I get on the bestseller list?* The magic vanishes. The joy dissipates. And it all seems impossible.

Now my dear Paula Munier is saying the magic words to us another way. Once upon a time, she begins. Once upon a time there was—you. And you wanted to create your unique story, and tell it beautifully, and you got a computer and sharpened your pencils and—then what? Let me tell you a story about your journey, she says, with that smile of hers. With its pitfalls and obstacles, its joys and beauty.

But we're no longer children, right? Not as eager to listen. Hurry hurry, we demand! Tell me the secret. What is it that you know, Paula, that we don't? Can't we just skim this? Can't we just look at the table of contents and skip to the conclusions? But that is Paula's secret, and I can reveal it to you right here: The only secret is unlocking the commitment and craft and passion within yourself. And page by page, without you even realizing it, this book will allow it to happen to you. (Go ahead, underline. Highlight. Flap down the corners of your special pages. I won't tell.)

As the chapters of this lovely book unfold, so will your writing life. Your skills and your surprises, the wonderful words that are just around the next corner. This book will allow you to get there. Peacefully. Simply. On your own. From the inside out.

I know this.

At one point while reading *Writing with Quiet Hands*, I began to feel … different. I paused, trying to assess. Was I about to cry? What was I noticing? And then I realized—it was peace. I was feeling peace. Paula's thoughtful, loving, and gently brilliant words were twisting like smoke wisps thought my brain, quieting and calming and infusing me with joy. And confidence.

I have to go write now. And you will want to as well. It's just that kind of a book.

Hank Phillippi Ryan

introduction

"Outside of a dog, a book is a man's best friend. Inside of a dog, it's too dark to read." —GROUCHO MARX

I must have been a lonely child. As the sole offspring of a military officer who was often away at war (among other classified activities) and his adoring military officer's wife, I spent my childhood in a lot of places. So many different places—from Georgia to Germany, Oklahoma to Ohio, and so on—that I cannot recall them all, much less answer those Internet security questions like "What street did you grow up on?" and "Who was your third-grade teacher?" My childhood memories are a blur of Army bases, foreign countries, and Mayflower moving vans.

I once heard actor Swoosie Kurtz—also a military brat and an only child—describe that predicament as the double whammy of loneliness, because you're always the new kid, with no friends at school and no siblings at home to soften the blow. And while that was as true for me as it was for her, I don't remember being lonely as a child. I remember being happy. And the reason I remember being happy, rather than lonely, is twofold: (1) my mother, who adored me as much as she adored my father, and (2) books.

Let's start with my mother, as therapists love to do when they find out I'm an only child. (When they find out I'm also an Army brat, well, that's a matter for another book.) Mom has always been a reserved person, and the transitory life of the military is tough on reserved people. Making new friends was never easy for her. The constant pressure to succeed in the snobbish social circles of officers' wives—a success critical to her husband's career path—forced her to assume an outgoing persona that was not hers by nature.

But my mother did not want me to suffer as she did, and so she taught me to be outgoing, whether I liked it or not. On the first day in a new neighborhood, she'd push me out the front door and tell me not to come home until I'd made a new friend. I'd wander the streets looking for children my age and then bribe one to come to my house with the promise of Pepsi and Pillsbury chocolate chip cookies—my 1960s mother's idea of the perfect snack.

Mom's soda-and-sweets trick worked every time, and I got better at making friends. But despite my growing skills in conviviality and coercion, I remained, like my mother, a bookworm at heart.

THE CONSOLATION OF STORY

Mom turned to reading for solace and solitude, for entertainment and enlightenment—and I learned to do the same. She read mysteries for escape and catalogs for clothes and decorating magazines for instruction on transforming the ugliest Army quarters into beautiful spaces. She even read esoterica for insomnia: When my dad was in Vietnam during the war, my mother was consumed with worry—and only the scholarly prose of *The Rise and Fall of the Third Reich* by William L. Shirer could lull her to sleep every night.

Mom never finished that monster three-and-a-half-pound tome, and when my dad came home she abandoned the book altogether. She went on to read a series of bestsellers about sex, most notably *The Sensuous Woman* by "J" and *Everything You Ever Wanted to Know About Sex, but Were Afraid to Ask* by Dr. David Reuben, both of which I found hidden under her pillow in the bed she shared with my father when I was a tween. *Gross,* I thought at the time, but I read them anyway.

My mother taught me that books could not only amuse and console, they could also teach me everything I ever wanted to know about anything—and I was never afraid to ask. I devoured the written word—fairy tales, myths and fables, novels old and new, nonfiction books on astronomy and archaeology and anthropology. I loved libraries, particularly school libraries where I could hide away from

writing with quiet hands

the disinterested classmates I felt charged to befriend. Each military post boasted a library as well, and unfortunately my mother's haphazard book-borrowing habits inevitably led to late fees. With typical military precision, the post library would send the dunning notices to my father's commanding officer, who would hand them to my father, along with a lecture on his inability to manage his wife.

So Mom preferred buying books to borrowing them. Always the vigilant curator of my young life, she disdained the comic books all the cool kids were reading—and wouldn't budge on that score. But I quickly learned that whenever I did ask for a twenty-five-cent comic book, she'd buy me a one-dollar Nancy Drew novel instead. Soon I had a small library to call my own. (Decades later, to mark the publication of my first book, my parents presented me with a handmade lamp symbolizing my career as a writer. The lampshade is a collage of my magazine and newspaper articles published to date, and the base is a stack of my favorite childhood books—including Helen Wells's *Cherry Ames: Student Nurse*, *Volume A* of the *World Book Encyclopedia,* and Desmond Morris's *The Naked Ape.*)

Like most children who grow up to be writers, I loved to read. I was a good reader. Grandpa Ed, my paternal grandfather, encouraged me. He taught fifth grade and was inordinately pleased that by the tender age of six I could read as well or better than any of his ten-year-old students. We didn't see Grandpa Ed often, as he lived in Indiana and we lived, well, everywhere else, but whenever we did see him, he brought me books. I still have the copy of the Hoosier classic *The Bears of Blue River* that he gave to me before he died when I was twelve.

But unlike most children who grow up to be writers, I didn't want to be a writer. I didn't know any writers. The only thing close to writers in my world were the soldiers who worked for the *Stars and Stripes* newspaper, and I don't have to tell you what my father, the Colonel, thought of them. Certainly we didn't associate with any writers—or any kind of artists, for that matter. Apart from the Army bands playing John Philip Sousa on Field Day, Memorial Day, Veterans Day, and the Fourth of July, there were no artists of any stripe to be found on the military bases where I grew up.

I didn't know any writers. And even if I had, I would never have believed that I could—or should—have been one of them.

PUTTING WORDS ON PAPER

But I did write. Not stories, other than what was required for my schoolwork. What I wrote were letters. Hundreds, maybe thousands, of letters, to the family and friends I was always leaving behind. In a time when there was no e-mail or text messaging, and long-distance phone calls were prohibitively pricey, letters were my way of holding onto my relationships as long as I could. But multiple moves, the vagaries of the United States Postal Service, and the inevitable passage of time and interest eroded my careful correspondence, and I lost touch with nearly everyone I knew when I was a child. (The notable exception was my Grandma Emma in Indiana, the one person I could always count on to write me back. Her correspondence read like a Hoosier's *Farmers' Almanac*—short on words but long on the weather and local flora and fauna, which taught me that setting is, indeed, everything.)

Most of us Army brats wrote letters, usually to no avail. But not always. When James, my best friend from seventh grade, tracked me down decades later, I was thrilled that he'd not only kept my letters but had also saved a copy of the literary journal we had worked on together as twelve-year-olds at the now-defunct Baumholder American High School in Germany. I still had some of his letters, too, but I'd forgotten about the literary journal, for which I'd served as editor.

"I always knew you'd be a writer," he told me when we met again for the first time in thirty years.

James may have known, but I didn't. And even when it became obvious, I resisted. Mrs. Berentz, my ninth-grade English teacher at George S. Patton Junior High School in Fort Leavenworth, Kansas, took it upon herself to call my mother and tell her directly that "you should encourage your daughter to be a writer." My mother, always quick to believe anyone who claimed that her only child was unique in any way, listened earnestly to Mrs. Berentz and began encouraging me as instructed, at least when my father wasn't around. The Colonel had other plans for me; he wanted me to be the Army's first female helicopter pilot. Neither option appealed to me. I was fourteen, and the last thing I wanted to do was what either of my parents wanted me to do.

And then everything changed. The Army sent us to New Orleans. Once there, my parents enrolled me in Ursuline Academy, an all-girls Catholic high school ruled by nuns.

I thought this was terrible, if not downright medieval—but I was wrong. It was NOLA, after all, a place rife with writers and artists and musicians—or, as my father called them, *civilians*. I loved this creative and chaotic environment, so different from military bases: *Laissez les bons temps roulez!*

I even loved the nuns, especially Sister Esther, a remarkable woman with a formidable intellect who taught me how to think—and then how to write down those thoughts in an organized and engaging way. She encouraged me to read widely—from Emerson and Thoreau to Voltaire and Shakespeare—and then challenged me to discuss those authors' works with her.

We spent two-and-a-half glorious years in the Crescent City—the most exciting years of my young life, and certainly the most influential in terms of my becoming a writer. Mrs. Berentz said I *could* be a writer, and she was *smart*, but Sister Esther said I *would* be a writer, and she was *brilliant*. But when the orders came in for Fort Benjamin-Harrison, we packed up again and moved to Indiana. Good soldier that I was, I went to my father's alma mater, Purdue University, to study geophysics (my dad's second choice for me, given the fact that my bookworm eyes weren't good enough for flight school). I hated it so much that I married my first husband.

Now I had something to write about. I quit Purdue to help put my husband through graduate school at Northwestern, working at a company that made cardboard boxes—which was nearly as exciting as it sounds. Broke and bored, I decided to make some extra cash by writing articles for periodicals. It was the late 1970s, and my favorite magazine was *Cosmopolitan*, then in its Helen Gurley Brown prime. I pounded out an 800-word story about "keeping your love alive" on my old manual typewriter and mailed the pages in an envelope with a SASE as instructed by *Writer's Digest* magazine. *Cosmopolitan* did not accept unsolicited material, but that didn't stop me. I had Mrs. Berentz and Sister Esther on my side.

A month later, I got a nice acceptance letter in the mail, along with a check from the Hearst Corporation for $50, which was about half a week's pay at the cardboard box company. I had sold the first article I ever wrote to one of the biggest magazines in the country. *Nothing to this writing business,* I thought.

I cashed the check, and I waited. Month after month, I checked the latest issue of the magazine for my story, and month after month, I was disappointed. I didn't write anything else, because I didn't need the money any more. My husband got a good job, and I got pregnant. We moved to Florida. The day we brought our newborn daughter, Alexis, home from the hospital, *Cosmo* arrived in the mail—and my article was in it. I had my first child *and* my first published story! Life was perfect.

Two babies and one divorce later, I was broke again. My ex-husband had disappeared with all our money, and I had kids to support. I needed a job, and I had neither a college degree nor any experience apart from that lackluster stint at the cardboard box company. I was qualified to do absolutely nothing. So armed with my *Cosmo* clip and a very creative cover letter and résumé, I talked my way into a job as an editorial assistant at a business magazine.

Now I was a real professional writer. All I had to do was learn to write.

THEY'RE GOING TO PAY ME FOR THIS?

The Colonel was worried that I'd crash and burn and that my children would starve. My mother was worried that I'd succeed but given my paltry pay—even worse than what the military offered—my children would starve anyway.

But what I lacked in talent and experience I made up for in luck. My editor at the business magazine was a magnanimous man named Tom Owens whose incredible editorial skill was equaled only by his incredible patience. I wrote and wrote, and he red-lined and red-lined. The affable and assiduous Mr. Owens taught me to write, one painstaking edit at a time.

Just as I got better at making friends, I got better at making stories. My military upbringing provided me with three of the traits most useful to a beginning writer: (1) discipline, (2) punctuality, and (3) a respect for rank. I worked hard, I met my deadlines, and I did whatever

Tom told me to do. By the time I left eighteen months later, I'd learned enough to talk my way into a job as the editor of a new business newspaper. (I've never actually interviewed for a job; I've just talked people into hiring me. It's a lot like talking kids into being my friends, minus Mom's Pepsi and Pillsbury chocolate chip cookies.)

When I showed the Colonel the debut issue of the business paper, he was dismayed. "Who else reads this before it goes to print?"

"No one," I said proudly.

"That's not right."

"Well, Dad, I *am* the editor."

His discomfort only grew when he realized that I was spending my nights and weekends writing my first novel. "Just finish it and get it out of your system," he told me.

I never sold that novel, but I did get it out of my system. It was good enough to get me my first agent—the inestimable Ethan Ellenberg— and to attract the attention of an editor, the beautiful and brainy Gail Greiner, who took it with her when she switched from adult fiction to young adult. She called me and asked if I'd ever considered writing for children. The main characters in my novel had been teenagers at the beginning of the story, and she thought that I "wrote teens well." Would I be interested in writing a YA novel for her?

Of course I would. She was creating a series for HarperCollins about American teenagers abroad. I was to pick a country and outline a plot. The first part was easy: I picked Ireland. The second part, not so much. I'd never outlined a novel before, having written my first one by the seat of my pants. Five drafts of that outline later, I'd won a contract to write *Emerald's Desire* and the right to complain about my publisher's title, which naturally I hated. Just like a real writer.

And that's how I felt: just like a real writer. Because despite the pleasure—and paychecks—I earned writing newspaper and magazine stories, in my mind, real writers wrote books. (Even the Colonel agreed with me there—and not only because I'd dedicated the book to him and Mom.)

Now I'd written a book, and I dared think of myself as a real writer, too. Even better, I'd talked my way into a job as managing editor for Prima Publishing (later acquired by Random House), an independent house that specialized in trade books as well as strategy guides for video games. At the first editorial meeting at Prima, I realized that they were going to pay me to read books and talk about them all day—and I nearly burst into tears.

I loved that job. So much so that when *Emerald's Desire* came out the same week I started at Prima, I barely noticed, having happily fallen victim to Editor's Syndrome. Or, as the legendary editor of *The Washington Post* Ben Bradlee put it: "Just as I was beginning to get good at writing, I became an editor."

I was consumed with the books of other writers: acquiring them, editing them, producing them, promoting them. I came up with ideas for books, I commissioned writers to write books, I edited books, I rewrote books, I proofread the final pages of books, I created jacket and catalog copy for books, I marketed books—I did everything with books except write my own.

And I loved every minute of it. I was the midwife to my writers' babies, shepherding hundreds of books a year into the hands of eager readers. By any measure, it was a lovely and rewarding way for a bookworm to spend her days.

No regrets—but when ten years had gone by without my writing another book, I jumped at the chance to write a little volume called *On Being Blonde.* I had thirty days to write it. Fortunately, it was a short book—but not so short that writing it in a month while juggling a full-time job and single motherhood wouldn't be a challenge. I was rusty, I was scared, I was more editor than writer. But I knew that I had to do it to save whatever writer was left in me before the Editor Borg took over completely.

I wrote that book in a month and never looked back. I continued my career as a publishing executive—from Quarto to Disney, Greenspun Media Group to F+W Media—but I also kept writing. When Gina Panettieri invited me to become an agent with Talcott Notch Literary, I took on the role of selling stories as well as telling them. In the process, I began teaching writing classes, passing on what Tom Owens and Gail Greiner and all my fellow editors and writers and agents taught me along the way. Teaching led to my first book on writing, *Plot Perfect: How to Build Unforgettable Stories Scene by Scene,* which I wrote in a state of wonder: Now they were paying me to write books *about* writing!

ONCE A WRITER ...

On my journey from reader to writer, editor, agent, and teacher, I've come to believe that writers are born, not made. Some of us who love reading and books are destined to become writers ourselves. Books are our friends—and that friendship becomes a happy marriage when we sit down to write our own stories.

Becoming a writer is not about becoming rich and famous any more than getting married is about becoming rich and famous—although that's why some people write and why some people get married. Even being a good writer does not guarantee riches and stardom—although it can't hurt. (And we all know how those marriages made in the name of fame and fortune turn out.)

Like any good marriage, being a writer requires care, commitment, and, perhaps above all else, a sense of calling. We are called to write, to shape our words into well-crafted stories, and to share those stories in the hope of embracing our experiences and illuminating our lives.

That's why I was called to write this book. Publishers need writers. Writers need readers. And readers need good stories. Learning to write your best stories is what this book is all about.

To paraphrase Mark Twain, the difference between a good story and a bad story is the difference between alone and lonely. They say that writing can be a lonely profession. But I don't believe that. The best stories keep the loneliness at bay for all of us, readers and writers alike.

Because, as I learned during my so-called lonely childhood, when you're alone with a good book, you're never lonely.

PART ONE

inspiration meets craft

in·spi·ra·tion

noun \ in(t)-spə-ˈrā-shən, -(ˌ)spi-\

: something that makes someone want to do something or that gives someone an idea about what to do or create

C.1300, "immediate influence of God or a god," especially that under which the holy books were written, from Old French *inspiracion* "inhaling, breathing in; inspiration," from Late Latin *inspirationem* (nominative *inspiratio*), noun of action from past participle stem of Latin *inspirare* "inspire, inflame, blow into," from in- "in" + spirare "to breathe"; literal sense "act of inhaling" attested in English from 1560s; meaning "one who inspires others" is from 1867

craft

noun \ˈkraft\

: an activity that involves making something in a skillful way by using your hands

Old English *cræft* "strength, power, skill," of Germanic origin; related to Dutch *kracht*, German *Kraft*, and Swedish *kraft* "strength, power"

CHAPTER ONE

a commitment to craft

"Would that my hands were meant to build. Then I would know what to say." —PIERCE BROWN

Quiet hands are sure hands, hands that know what they are doing. They're the light hands of the accomplished equestrienne, calmly holding the reins of a thoroughbred longing to leap. They are the strong hands of a Taekwondo master, striking a steep stack of solid bricks. And they are the supple hands of the craftsperson, skillfully shaping raw material into artful form. The sculptor at her marble. The whittler at his wood. The potter at her wheel.

The best writers are quiet-handed craftspeople, too. Novelist Isaac Asimov attributed his prolific output to quiet hands on the keys, "thinking through my fingers." Songwriter Paul Simon aims to write with quiet hands while holding "a humble pen." Poet Mary Oliver wrote specifically about her desire to write with quiet hands in her poem "Everything." *

They know that craft matters as much as inspiration—maybe more. Inspiration is the spark that lights the fire of story—but it is craft that burns away all its imperfections and hardens the glaze to a glorious shine. I once heard a potter complain that she disliked the glazing part of the process because of its ability to make or break a perfectly good pot. The same is true for story. Poor craftsmanship can ruin a perfectly good sto-

---

* From *New and Selected Poems, Volume Two* by Mary Oliver

ry idea, yet good craftsmanship can transform that perfectly good story idea into a classic—and salable—work.

As a writer, I've suffered the frustration that comes when you are not sure how to shape your raw material into artful form. As an editor and a writing teacher, I've helped writers master the tools and techniques that can polish their work to a glorious shine. And as a literary agent, I've learned the hard way that nothing spells "no sale" faster than a broken pot. It's the marriage of inspiration and craft that translates into sales.

Writing with quiet hands is the secret to creating stories that resonate with agents, editors, publishers, and, ultimately, readers. When you write with quiet hands, you won't make the mistake too many of your fellow writers make: You won't try to sell your manuscript before it's truly ready for prime time. With this simple three-part primer, you'll discover how to manifest your inspiration, master the finer points of writing, and lay the groundwork for marketing your work.

Whether you're just beginning your writer's journey or you're a seasoned storyteller looking to refine your artistry, you'll learn the subtleties of creation, composition, and craft that can make the difference between published and unpublished work.

Let's get started.

"Aim for a deep seat and quiet hands."
—JEANNE GRUNERT

WHY CRAFT MATTERS

P.G. Wodehouse once said that the worst thing about being a beginning writer was that you had no idea how bad you were. But we are all beginners at the outset, and even as we master the craft we tend to challenge ourselves by taking on more demanding projects. Craft begets craft—and what you learn while writing one story may or may not be enough to write the next. Being a good writer means approaching craft as an iterative process that refines and deepens your work over a lifetime.

When you open a book by your favorite writer and begin to read, from the very first line you know you are in good hands. You relax, sigh with pleasure, and think, *I'm in for a great ride.* And you sit back to enjoy a reading experience that will prove worthy of the several hours and dollars you're investing in that story.

One of my favorite writers is Alice Hoffman. She's a master storyteller whose stories often read as postmodern fairy tales, told in a style she calls "Yankee magic realism." But her fans don't care what it's called; they know it when they read the first line of her stories. Here's a sampling of strong first lines from some of Hoffman's books, listed in no particular order:

> Be careful what you wish for.
>
> *—The Ice Queen*

> I was born out of sorrow, so my mother named me Rain.
>
> *—The Foretelling*

> It was earthquake weather, and everyone knew it.
>
> *—Fortune's Daughter*

> For more than two hundred years, the Owens women have been blamed for everything that has gone wrong in town.
>
> *—Practical Magic*

> Once a year there was a knock on the door.
>
> *—The Story Sisters*

> It was said that boys should go on their first sea voyage at the age of ten, but surely this notion was never put forth by anyone's mother.
>
> *—Blackbird House*

> We had been wandering for so long I forgot what it was like to live within walls or sleep through the night.
>
> *—The Dovekeepers*

> Anyone born and bred in Massachusetts learns early on to recognize the end of winter.
>
> *—The Probable Future*

Every time I buy a new Alice Hoffman story—and I buy them all—I settle down on my couch with a cup of tea and a smile, and open to the first page. I read the first line, and I fall into what John Gardner called "the fictive dream." Hoffman's ability to drop me into her world from the opening line is why I keep coming back for more, year after year, book after book.

That's the authority of craft. Well-crafted stories are a joy to read, deliver on the promise of a good reading experience from the first word, and, most important, help you build a loyal audience who will sustain your writing career through praise and pans, bestsellers and bombs, good times and bad.

A QUESTION OF CRAFT

Which writers do you think of when you think of craft? Whose first lines drop you right into the fictive dream, time and again? How does their craftsmanship inform your reading experience?

IT'S ALL IN YOUR READER'S HEAD

The best reading experiences literally change the brains of readers. According to the findings of a recent Emory University study published in the journal *Brain Connectivity*, when you get caught up in a book, your brain gets caught up, too. Compelling stories heighten connectivity in the reader's left temporal cortex—a part of the brain related to language and sensory motor skills—and trigger neurological changes that can endure, much as muscle memory does. Which means that when you craft a compelling read, you're affecting your readers' brains in a powerful way. What's more, create a sympathetic hero and your readers put themselves in his shoes. Their brains trick them into believing that they are walking your protagonist's walk and talking your protagonist's talk— not just figuratively but *biologically* as well. It's the same phenomenon runners experience when they think about running— and thereby activate the neurons in their brains related to the physical act of running. In the study, these neurological changes were still in effect five days after subjects finished reading, leading researchers to believe that well-crafted stories can have a lasting influence on their readers' brains. And they say being a writer isn't brain surgery. No, it's bigger than that. It's brain *science*!

Craft is the writer's *tell*—what gamblers call the mannerisms and gestures and other subconscious signals that reveal whether a poker player has a good or a bad hand. Craft is made up of the voice and plot and other fictive elements that reveal whether a writer has a good or bad story. Readers know it when they see it—just as gamblers do.

(If you're wondering how I know so much about gambling, it's not because I'm a gambler; at one time I was the editor of *Las Vegas Weekly*. We did a lot of stories about gambling, the fuel that fires Sin City. I am too cheap to gamble; as soon as I lose enough to buy a pretty pair of shoes I am officially pissed off. The biggest gamble I ever took was a career in publishing. Maybe it's your biggest gamble, too.)

Whether you are conscious of it or not, every word you write is a tell. That's why it's so important that you master your craft: so that your tell reveals to readers that yours is a story worth reading. Just as Alice Hoffman reveals with every word she writes, starting from the first page.

WRITE IT DOWN

Get a pen and some paper, and set a timer for five minutes. Write about what the word *craft* means to you and how it applies to your writing.

In my writing workshops, the students are always comparing themselves to one another, rating each other's work accordingly, and wondering who from the class will become my next client. Eventually one of the brasher writers will take me aside and ask the one question I dread: "Who among us is most likely to get published?"

At this point, I repeat the question for the benefit of the entire group, so I only have to answer the question once that day. Even so, no one ever likes my answer because (1) it is a truth many are not willing to hear and (2) they think I'm avoiding the question.

But I'm not avoiding the question at all. The truth is—and this is what I tell them—I don't know. And I don't know because there are too many variables, even before I factor in the vagaries of the publishing business itself. The variables related to craft alone make it impossible for me to predict accurately who the next published writer in any given group will be.

Why Talent Isn't Enough

Oh, you say, but that's easy. Just pick the most talented writer in the workshop.

If only talent were enough. Unfortunately it's not. Some of the most talented writers I know never fulfill their promise. They never finish or they never revise or they simply burn out or break down or move on to other pursuits. In other words, they never become craftspeople; they remain, as Hollywood would say, the talent. Talent may work in Hollywood, but in publishing the writers who make it big are those who (1) finish, (2) revise, and (3) keep on finishing and revising. In other words, they're the writers who harness their talent to the plow of craft—and keep on tilling the soil, no matter how hard the row to hoe.

We all know fabulously talented writers, musicians, and artists who, for whatever reason—a crisis of confidence, a lack of discipline, a descent into substance abuse—fail to persist in their efforts long enough to master their craft and find an audience. Or they do master their craft and find an audience—only to perish on the rocks of fame and fortune.

Others take detours and end up supporting the work rather than creating it themselves; these are the publishers and the producers, the editors and the agents, the publicists and the critics, the booksellers and the gallery owners, the teachers and the workshop leaders. They leave their dreams at other people's altars. Not that there's anything wrong with that—but I believe we lose a lot of talented artists that way.

The British have a saying: "Talent will out." But I cannot say with any certainty that talent will out, at least not on my side of the pond. Because talent, without the commitment to craft, is not enough.

Why a Great Story Idea Is Not Enough Either

In Hollywood, a great idea for a story—what the pros like to call "high concept"—can be enough to sell a treatment or a screenplay. They'll buy it just for the idea—and then hire a "real writer" to write the screenplay. That's because you can't copyright an idea, so they are happy to buy the rights to your good idea and then execute it however they like.

It doesn't work that way in publishing. If you are writing books, a great idea is just that—a great idea. The execution of that great idea is what matters—what publishers are willing to pay for—and that's where craft comes in.

I participate in a lot of pitching workshops, in which I help writers refine the pitches they'll use to query agents, editors, and publishers about their projects, in the hope of getting said projects published. The goal is to write a pitch that presents a writer's story in the most appealing light—persuading an agent, editor, or publisher that the idea is compelling enough to hold its own in a very competitive marketplace.

A healthy competition reigns at these workshops, as the participants evaluate the relative strength of their story ideas and tweak them to highlight their commercial viability. It's an exciting time, not only for the writers but also for me as an agent. Especially for me as an agent.

A solid pitch, after all, is the currency of my trade. My job as an agent is to sell my clients' work—and pitching is a critical part of this process. The point of the pitch is to interest editors in the story—so much so that they'll devote a couple of nights or an entire weekend to reading it. (Yes, editors and agents alike do the bulk of their reading in their so-called free time.)

Clients often blame me when their work doesn't sell. But that blame can be misplaced. If I've done my part, I've pitched a given story idea well enough to prompt editors to read it. Once the work is in an editor's hands, the reading begins. If the execution of the idea fails to live up to the promise of the pitch, then the editor passes and there's no sale.

Usually my pitch isn't to blame—it's the failure of the writer to execute on that good idea—a failure typically due to a lack of craft.

A great idea gets you read. A great idea well executed—a.k.a. craft—gets you published.

That's why, when I hear a great story idea I think I can pitch successfully, I am thrilled—but only up to a point. I know that a great idea is only half the battle—and too many writers who charge into the fray with a high-concept premise later fall as the fight drags on and their poor craftsmanship catches up with them. Another good idea dead in the water. Another project doomed to fail. Another disappointment for all concerned: writer, agent, and editor.

DRILL IT DOWN

For films, trailers are the equivalent of story idea pitches (or jacket copy). Think about the last movie you saw that disappointed you. Do you remember the trailer? Watch it again. Did a flawed execution of that idea, as pitched in the trailer, contribute to your disappointment? How so? Now consider the last book that disappointed you in a similar way. Why were you disappointed? When did that disappointment begin to set in? How did that disappointment relate to the idea and/or the execution of that idea?

All of this disappointment stemmed from the fact that the writer did not master the craft of writing. I have some clients who are screenwriters and playwrights who find the transition from screen and stage to the page challenging. They resist revising the work before I shop it, because in Hollywood, producers, directors, and even actors all give the writer notes. Like it or not, the writer must rewrite accordingly. The same goes for the playwright, for whom the rehearsal process serves as one long revision before the play opens—and even then the notes continue as the writer tweaks the play based on audience reaction. So these writers want to wait on feedback from the editors before they revise.

"Tell the editors I'll be happy to make any changes they want," they tell me.

writing with quiet hands

But that's not how it goes in book publishing. Acquisitions editors—the people responsible for acquiring projects for publishing houses—are looking for stories that are so well-crafted they need only minimal revision. This insistence on a high level of craft is seen by some writers as proof that "editors don't edit anymore" (a belief that I have found to be completely groundless, by the way). Rather, this high bar reflects the publishing professionals' desire to honor the vision of the author. They don't want to fix your "nearly there" story; they want to publish your "ready to rock the reader's world" story.

I learned this the hard way. As an editor, I'd acquired all kinds of fiction and nonfiction projects for various publishers over the course of nearly twenty years. Many of these were how-to projects authored by experts rather than writers—therapists writing self-help books, chefs writing cookbooks, entrepreneurs writing business books, etc. These people were not professional writers, and so as their editor I either paired them with co-authors or ghostwriters, or I rewrote their work myself.

When I became an agent, I took on some clients who needed the same kind of help with their novels and memoirs. I was still thinking like an editor instead of an agent. I realized that about six months in, when I served on a panel of agents at a writers conference with the engaging and supersmart agent Jason Yarn. When a writer in the audience asked him about what he was looking for, he said that he was looking for projects that were at least 90 percent there.

"Publishers want projects that are at least 95 percent there, so I can help you make up that 5 percent," Yarn said. "But no more."

A lightbulb went off in my head. I'd been taking on some projects that were only 50 to 75 percent there, thinking that I could make up the gap myself. But that was the editor in me talking—not the agent. Now I sign only writers who accept the fact that the bar is very high in publishing—and who are willing to master their craft to meet that bar.

THOSE WHO COMMIT, CRAFT

"I wanted to write stories for myself. At first it was purely an aesthetic thing about craft. I just wanted to become good at the art of something. And writing was very private." —AMY TAN

Okay, so maybe you're thinking this all sounds a little formidable, even depressing. But don't be discouraged. Another reason I never can predict who, in any given group of writers, will get published is because sometimes it's the least likely person.

You can never count anyone out. Long after the most talented writers have come and gone, the woman in the corner who struggles to put two words together, peppers my lectures with questions that everyone in the class (including me) considers sophomoric, and writes stories with no style or plot or even point in sight surprises everyone and gets published. She does it by continuing to write and revise, learn and revise, revise and revise. She takes craft seriously and puts in the hours and days and weeks and months and years it may take her to master that craft. She persists—and she gets published.

Fifteen years ago I moved to Salem, Massachusetts, about half an hour north of Boston. I missed the writers' group I'd left behind in California, so I organized a new one, inviting some writers I'd met at a meeting for the New England chapter of the Mystery Writers of America to come to my house weekly to share their work. This was a group made up primarily of refined and cultured women of very erudite tastes, most of whom were writing literary thrillers and drawing room mysteries.

And then there was Vaughn.

Vaughn was a U.S. Marine vet with a manner as subtle as an M16 assault rifle. The writing reflected the man. His very presence—not to mention his writing—offended the sensibilities of his fellow writers. Every week he came to the writers' group, and every week they picked apart his work as keenly and cleanly as vultures feeding on a wounded wildebeest. But he kept coming to the group, and he kept working. He wrote story after story, both long and short, and he revised them all many times. He went to writers conferences and classes, and he studied the work of his favorite writers.

He got better. He published a few of his short stories. He kept working.

writing with quiet hands

When Vaughn found out I was thinking of becoming an agent, he called me from his home in northern Maine. "Guess who your first client is?"

I laughed. "I give up."

"Me," he said.

I signed Vaughn, and he sent me his latest crime novel. I had him work on revisions, and when the story was ready, we shopped it. We sold the thriller in record time, and it debuted in 2014 to good reviews and brisk sales. Nominated for a major literary award, the book was even chosen for display at the Hudson News airport bookstores—a significant coup for a debut novel by an unknown writer. (Look for *Sniper* by Vaughn Hardacker wherever you buy your books.) Vaughn's second novel, *The Fisherman*, was published in June 2015, and his third is set to release in 2016.

If you'd asked any of his fellow writers in the group if they thought Vaughn would ever get published, they'd most likely have told you no. A polite but unequivocal no.

If you'd asked me, I would have reserved my judgment. Because then, as now, I know there's no predicting who will master the craft of writing. It may not be who you think it will be.

But if you commit to craft, it could be you.

VOLUNTARY APPRENTICESHIP

"We are all apprentices in a craft where no one ever becomes a master." —ERNEST HEMINGWAY

If you want to write and publish commercial fiction or creative nonfiction, you have to take charge of your own education. Sure, you can get a degree in English literature, but that will teach you how to deconstruct stories, not invent them. You can become a journalist, which many writers have done (myself included), but that will teach you how to write nonfiction from an unbiased (more or less) point of view, not how to write fiction or creative nonfiction. You can get an MFA, but that will teach you how to write short stories for literary journals that mostly pay in copies.

Which is not altogether a bad thing. Any discipline that requires writing, whether you're penning law briefs or press releases or news stories or literary criticism or technical manuals, provides valuable practice putting words together. It's akin to a pianist playing scales every day. That said, playing scales doesn't teach you how to compose a song or a symphony.

What's more, there's a danger in playing the scales for any length of time, because you'll acquire habits that you'll have to unlearn in order to become the best storyteller you can be. Journalists, trained to keep themselves out of the story and to focus only on a straightforward delivery of the facts, have to leave those strictures behind and learn the art of dramatization, of writing fully realized scenes, of layering image and theme and metaphor, of poetic license, and of fully exercising their imagination. When I was a reporter, I prided myself on writing tightly edited, lean, objective stories. But when I started writing fiction, I had to learn how to throw in everything but the kitchen sink, including whatever I'd been trained to edit out as a journalist. I had to figure out how to write from the inside out—which required completely shifting my writing gears.

In order to write fiction, technical writers need to abandon all jargon. Marketing writers need to forget spin and tell the unvarnished truth, warts and all. Attorneys need to embrace the freedom of telling stories unbound by the points of law. Critics need to turn off analysis and turn on invention. Screenwriters often need to relearn point of view, to develop an individual voice, and to build out scenes, just as playwrights need to rethink setting and action, and to reduce their dependence on dialogue.

Mastering the craft of story requires serving a voluntary apprenticeship of your own making. This is an apprenticeship devoted to craft so you can learn your trade as a writer. And even writers who've learned enough to get their stories published must continue to serve this apprenticeship to ensure that each new book is better than the last—not to mention to survive the inevitable ups and downs of a career in publishing.

One Million Words

"I wanted to be a writer, and I wrote." —Paulo Coelho

According to conventional wisdom, it takes one million words to make a writer. Becoming a writer, in effect, requires a million-word apprenticeship.

I first heard this from a writer in California nearly thirty years ago. I'd taken an adult education class in creative writing at the local community college, taught by the clever and compassionate Jon Kennedy. I had small children at the time, and so when the class ended I talked several of my classmates into forming a writers' group that would meet at my house once a week.

(Single parents, take note: Offer your home as the setting for your writers' group and you won't have to worry about getting a babysitter. Just train your children to go to bed early. You should train them to do this anyway, because kids need a good night's sleep and you need quiet time to write. Put the money you save on babysitters towards the writers conference of your choice.)

The most experienced writer in our group, apart from Jon, was a sociology professor who taught at the state university and had published several pieces in prestigious literary journals. She was smart and articulate, and she scared the hell out of me. When she said it took a million words to become a writer, I did the math in my head—and came up some 950,000 words short.

That impossible million-word target didn't seem to faze anyone else in the group. So I kept my mouth shut and kept writing unpublishable short stories. These were truly bad stories inspired by everyone else's experience but my own. One particularly terrible tale described an American soldier in Vietnam slicing ears off his slain enemies and preserving them in pickle jars. (I told you they were terrible.)

But I was as determined as I was clueless. I produced one new story every week, and the pages piled up. By the end of the year, I was 100,000 words closer to my million-word mark. I figured I'd written a novel's worth of unpublishable short stories, so I might as well write an unpublishable novel. I wasn't a big fan of short stories and hadn't read that many, other than those required in school. As a reader, I'd always preferred the novel. So I switched to novels and continued my trek to the one-million-word mark.

Whether you've yet to put pen to paper or have already racked up 999,999 words, you always have more to learn. Malcolm Gladwell says that it takes ten thousand hours of practice to become truly proficient at anything—and maybe he's right. But some writers write very slowly—and others write very quickly. (Do you hate those people? I hate those people.) Donna Tartt takes ten years or more to write a novel; the late, great Robert B. Parker wrote at least three novels a year, one for each of his series, along with his Virgil Cole books and his stand-alone stories. (I don't hate Bob Parker; I loved him *and* his Spenser and Jesse and Sunny.) Of course, Tartt's last book, *The Goldfinch,* is nearly eight hundred pages long, and Bob Parker's books run far shorter.

Still, given the varying speeds at which writers work, the one-million-word goal is more apt than ten thousand hours. And maybe easier to reach: You only have to write one hundred words an hour to hit the one-million-word mark in ten thousand hours.

If you're thinking, *Hold on, it's not that simple: A computer can "write" a million words in milliseconds, and no one would want to read that,* you'd be right. There's more to good storytelling than mere words. Words are the clay; the story is the pot.

Hand in Hand with Inspiration

This brings us full circle, back to writing with quiet hands. This is how master craftspeople work: confident, competent, creative hands producing confident, competent, creative work. Practice—those one million words—can help you achieve a certain level of competency. As your competency grows, so may your confidence. But without creativity, all the competency and confidence in the world will only take you so far. Not as far as you need to go to get published. Not as far as you want to go to become the writer you were born to be. Certainly not as far as the bestseller list.

The best apprenticeship is a program that increases your competency, builds your confidence, and revs up your creativity. This holy trinity of good writing—competency, confidence, and creativity—are the keys to writing with quiet hands. Together they not only make the difference between a good writer and a bad writer, they make the difference between a good writer and a truly exceptional one.

The best work is the result of a happy marriage of craft and inspiration. If you've made it this far in the book, you've made your commitment to craft. Now it's time to ask inspiration to join the party—by courting your muse.

HANDS ON

Every apprentice needs a master craftsman. Consider the craftspeople you know who work with their hands—sculptors, carpenters, painters, composers, quilters, even poets—and choose one or two with whom you can talk about craft. Ask them how they got started, what their apprenticeship was like, how the lessons learned during their apprenticeship inform their work today, and what working with quiet hands means to them. If possible, observe them—and their hands—at work. Take notes.

CHAPTER TWO

the taming of the muse

"... happy is he whom the Muses love: sweet flows speech from his mouth." —HESIOD

When it comes to courting the muse, writers are as superstitious as baseball players. Rituals and icons and talismans abound, all designed to stay on the good side of the muse, who when pleased will let you go with the flow, fire up your imagination, and ward off potential evils, like flat prose and plot holes and writer's block.

Leo Tolstoy and Friedrich Nietzsche both insisted that the best way to summon the muse is to take a walk. William Burroughs wrote down all his dreams because he believed that his muse visited him while he was asleep. Ken Kesey's muse was William Faulkner, whom he read to "get going" when he sat down to write.

Some writers beckon the muse with beauty: Amy Tan places historical artifacts related to her work in progress on her desk; Alice Hoffman paints her writing room the color that resonates with her current project. Others rely on particular tools: John Steinbeck used only round pencils—not hexagonal ones—and Elmore Leonard wrote all his novels on legal pads. And, perhaps most famously, many writers lured the muse with liquor: Tennessee Williams said he couldn't write without wine, and Norman Mailer needed a can of beer "to prime" himself. In fact, so many writers have relied upon plying the muse with booze that alcoholism has often been called "the writer's disease."

Then there are the writers who refuse to acknowledge the muse at all. (You know these people—they're the ones who are always quoting Thomas A. Edison: "Genius is 1 percent inspiration and 99 percent perspiration.") There's no such thing as inspiration, they'll tell you. Or if there is, there's no relying on it. The muse, if she exists at all, is viewed as a fickle creature, as likely to sabotage good work as to bless it.

Even if you don't believe in the muse, there's no point in going out of your way to piss her off, just in case you're wrong. She's kind of like God in that way.

While you may view all these muse-related rites and remedies as so much nonsense, you can't deny—Edison aside—that inspired work is work that stirs the hearts of editors, agents, and readers as well. In short, inspired work sells. So let's take a look at how you can draw on inspiration as you master your craft.

FEEDING THE BEAST

"I learned that you should feel when writing, not like Lord Byron on a mountain top, but like a child stringing beads in kindergarten—happy, absorbed and quietly putting one bead on after another."
—BRENDA UELAND

Woodcrafters know that it's not enough to build something well—the most successful pieces are beautiful *and* well built. Form is as important as function.

Marry form and function, and you can create a story that's as beautiful and well built as a Shaker rocking chair. The Shakers, whose furniture represents perhaps the ultimate expression of form meeting function, considered the construction of each piece an act of prayer inspired by the grace of God.

You may not consider your writing an act of prayer, or call upon the grace of God or the blessing of the muse to inspire you, but if you do, you are honoring the very meaning of the word *inspiration*, which comes from the Latin *inspiratio,* meaning "breath of God (or god)" or "divine guidance."

For best results, however, you need to define your god or muse. An angry, vengeful, Old Testament kind of God or a scolding harpie kind of muse will not serve your work well—and may shut down your creativity completely. What you need is a little fun.

You read that right. *Fun.* If you are not having fun with your writing, if you find writing torturous and soul killing, then you should do something else. The same is true if you are writing to become rich and famous. There are far less stressful and taxing paths to fame and fortune. If you're in the writing game to make money, quit now—and take up investment banking. If you're in the writing game to become a household name, quit now—and pull a Kim Kardashian.

The only reason to be a writer is because (1) you love writing and/or (2) you couldn't stop writing even if you tried—and you've already tried. If the latter applies to you, then you need to learn to enjoy the process. You need to make it fun. It *needs* to be fun. Or, at the very least, engrossing. That's what inspiration is all about.

If you're not engaging yourself, how can you possibly expect to engage the reader? If you're not amusing yourself, how can you possibly expect to amuse the reader? If you're not entertaining yourself, how can you possibly expect to entertain the reader?

What's the most fun you ever had while writing? Be honest. If you're one of those writers who *never* has any fun while writing, think again. Sometimes the most enjoyable writing experiences are those that are not part of your career plan. The most fun I've had recently while writing was preparing the instructions for a contest at the New England Crime Bake. I was the banquet chair, in charge of entertainment, and given the fact that our guest of honor was the wonderful Craig Johnson, author of the Sheriff Walt Longmire series, I decided that we'd run a (Dead) Cowboy Poetry Contest for all of the mystery writers in attendance. So I wrote up the rules in light verse:

(DEAD) COWBOY POETRY CONTEST RULES

Tonight all you wordslingers
Must earn your own chow.

So sit down with your table posse
For a little powwow.
Pen a (dead) cowboy poem
Worthy of the Wild, Wild West.
(We know you're really New Englanders,
So just do your best.)
Remember, the cowboy must die
Without losing his boots.
Double score for lingua franca
Like *yep*, *soirée*, and *cahoots*.
A couplet, a sonnet, even
A limerick will do.
And yes, it must rhyme,
Unless you opt for haiku.
In which case Sheriff Longmire
May just arrest you.
You've got twenty minutes—
Hell, we've killed real men in far less.
So get a move on, little doggies
You've got Judge Johnson to impress!

Ridiculous, I know, but I had a great time writing this and was inordinately proud of it—a pride in which I felt justified when the estimable Hallie Ephron called me brilliant. More important, the writing of this silly ditty prompted an afternoon's solid work on my novel in progress.

WRITE IT DOWN

Get a pen and some paper, and set the timer for seven minutes. Write about the most fun you ever had while writing. Be honest.

By having some fun first, I tricked my subconscious—the true god of the imagination—into coming out to play. You can do the same thing once you understand the nature of the brain and how to harness it to work for you rather than against you.

STORMING YOUR BRAIN

"Writing is so much damned fun. I play God. I feel like a kid at Christmas. I make people do what I want, and I change things as I go along." —TOM CLANCY

Whether you believe that God (or some universal force) took six days or millions of years to create the Earth, you have to admit that, from a storyteller's point of view, it looks like the guy had a good time doing it. What an imagination: He created an amazing setting with deserts and mountains and swamps and seas and storms and earthquakes and germs and bugs and mammals and Cro-Magnon man, and then he threw in some plot elements like evolution and ice ages. Finally he gave our Homo sapiens hero—or is he the villain?—free will and curiosity and seemingly equal, if conflicting, propensities for generosity and violence. Then he sat back and let the fur fly. Look at the world we live in—this is a world created by a playful God worthy of the act of creation.

Are you a playful God worthy of the act of creation? Playing God is the writer's job. We all think we'd like to be God—and daydream about what life would be like were we really in charge of the universe. If I were the boss of you and everything else, there'd be no fast food and no parking meters, and there'd be more librarians than lawyers and more poets than politicians and free Wi-Fi and college and yoga for everyone and … . See? That sounds great, until the responsibility of it hits us. What's to be done about war and world hunger and that wastrel down the street who refuses to clean up his yard?

Deciding who lives and who dies in our stories is just part of that responsibility—a duty that can stop us in our tracks, leading to sleepless nights, unfinished manuscripts, and very expensive therapy sessions. But playing God can also be fun—provided your imagination is fully on board.

The playful god is the one who happily creates entire worlds from scratch, selecting the setting, peopling it with all kinds of characters and creatures, good and bad, and subjecting them all to feast and famine, love and war, death and dinosaurs, and disasters both natural and unnatural. He's the philologist who designs Middle-earth down to the smallest detail—from the exquisitely intricate cartography to the extravagant cast of dragons, dwarves, hobbits, elves, men, orcs, wizards, and wargs to the numerous complex languages spoken by the aforementioned denizens of his fictive dream (J.R.R. Tolkien). She's the American scientist from Arizona who imagines a smart and sexy genre-bending historical science-fiction adventure-romance epic about an English ex-combat nurse in postwar northern Britain who is propelled back to eighteenth-century Scotland, where she finds herself caught in the middle of the ongoing skirmishes between the ruling English and the rebellious Highland Scots (Diana Gabaldon).

A QUESTION OF CRAFT

When it comes to playing God, who are your favorite writers? What about their world building excites you? *Note:* Don't think only in terms of science fiction writers and historical fiction writers. Think also of Jodi Picoult and her everyday American protagonists in extraordinary circumstances, Carl Hiaasen and his comic take on crime, or Judy Blume and her poignant re-creation of childhood.

Seducing Your Subconscious

"The creation of something new is not accomplished by the intellect but by the play instinct acting from inner necessity. The creative mind plays with the objects it loves. … Without this playing with fantasy, no creative work has ever yet come to birth. The debt we owe to the play of the imagination is incalculable." —CARL JUNG

As we've seen, writers will resort to some interesting and sometimes intense means of inviting the muse to bless their work. Thanks to ongoing developments and discoveries in brain science, we can avail ourselves of certain techniques that can put us in touch with our subconscious mind, the veritable playground of the storytelling gods, home to our intuition, emotions, dreams, memories, the collective unconscious, and more.

I've always envied visual artists because they seem to have a direct line to their subconscious. From where I sit as a writer, it looks like they just show up at the studio and plug right into their unconscious minds—and out it pours onto the canvas. Think of Jackson Pollock dribbling and drabbling paint at will, subconsciously re-creating the fractal patterns of nature years before fractals were discovered. I once spent an entire afternoon in front of Pollock's *One: Number 31, 1950* at the Museum of Modern Art, gazing at the work in silent reverence and watching people from all over the world seek it out and gaze along with me.

They say that writing is the most difficult of the arts because it does not appeal directly to a sense. Music appeals directly to our sense of hearing, painting to our sense of sight, the culinary arts to our senses of smell and taste, the textile arts to our sense of touch. When practitioners of these sense-related arts play—Miles Davis jamming on the trumpet, Martha Graham choreographing a dance, Chef Emeril Lagasse "takin' it up a notch" in the kitchen, Christo and Jeanne-Claude stringing saffron flags from 7,503 gates in New York City's Central Park—they can count on directly appealing to the senses of their audience in a way writers cannot.

Writing must undergo a translation in the reader's brain before it can be processed and understood. Typically the writer produces a series of black symbols on a white surface—letters on a page or screen—which must be interpreted by the reader. With any luck, that interpretation corresponds closely to the meaning the writer intended. This extra step puts us writers at a distance from our audience—a distance that other artists do not have to take into account.

All the more reason we should capitalize on our subconscious minds when we write. Here are some techniques that may help you:

- **TAKE A WALK.** The writers who begin their day's work with a long walk are too numerous to list here, but you can count Julia Cameron, Henry David Thoreau, and Jean-Jacques Rousseau among them. What's more, three forty-minute walks a week can actually grow your hippocampus, the part of your brain that forms, stores, and organizes your memories, according to a recent study by the University of Pittsburgh.
- **WARM UP.** You can warm up your writing muscles by entertaining your muse, just as the warm-up band entertains the audience before the concert headliner takes the stage. Try doing a crossword puzzle, writing a letter, or penning a haiku. For me, writing light verse—à la "(Dead) Cowboy Poetry Rules"—works every time.
- **MEDITATE.** Meditation enhances creativity—and creativity is your muse at work. Meditate for thirty-five minutes before you sit down to write, and you'll experience a boost in both divergent thinking (generating new ideas) and convergent thinking (focusing on solving one problem at a time), according to a recent study by Leiden University. Both divergent and convergent thinking are critical to good storytelling. Storytellers who have benefited from meditation include Kurt Vonnegut and Alice Walker.
- **SOUND IT OUT.** Music benefits the brain as well; studies show that listening to music can make you happier, relieve anxiety and depression, and activate the parts of the brain involved in movement, memory, planning, and attention, according to recent studies cited in *Trends in Cognitive Science*. Charles Bukowski listened to classical music on the radio as he wrote; Hunter Thompson preferred The Rolling Stones. Whatever floats your muse.
- **PLAY IT OUT.** If you play an instrument, all the better. Playing an instrument regularly boosts what is called the brain's executive functioning, which includes problem-solving skills and the ability to focus, say researchers at Boston Children's Hospital. The most famous writer band—or perhaps the only writer band—is

probably the Rock Bottom Remainders, whose members include Stephen King, Amy Tan, Dave Barry, and Mitch Albom.

- **USE YOUR HANDS.** Writing by hand boasts cognitive benefits that typing does not, according to a growing number of studies from such venerable institutions as the University of Washington, Indiana University, and Duke University. The finger movements involved in handwriting turn on the parts of the brain related to language, memory, thinking, and idea generation. Many writers always keep legal pads or index cards close at hand, on which they scribble notes for their works in progress. I have a big sketch notebook for each project, in which I jot down notes, draw maps, create family trees, plot out storylines, and paste pictures of characters and houses and whatever else my stories need. I use pens and pencils, colored pencils and magic markers, sticky notes and paper clips. The more toys, the better, as far as your subconscious is concerned.

- **SLEEP ON IT.** Anticipation can be half the fun. When you're sleeping, your conscious mind goes dormant, too—but your subconscious mind remains awake. Before you go to sleep, ruminate about your characters, the storyline, those big scenes you've yet to write. Get your subconscious excited about your story—and then let it do the work while you get a good night's rest, just like John Steinbeck liked to do.

Note: For more on writing and your brain, see *Fire Up Your Writing Brain* by Susan Reynolds.

THREE NO-BRAINER RULES FOR YOUR BRAIN

1. KEEP IT REAL. The subconscious mind cannot distinguish between reality and visualization. So when you visualize yourself sitting down to write every afternoon at 3 P.M. or pounding out ten pages every night or plotting a thriller with more twists and turns than Hitchcock, your subcon-

writing with quiet hands

scious believes you—so make your visualizations as true to life as possible.

2. **KEEP IT SIMPLE.** Your brain can focus best on only one habit at a time. So if you are focused on summoning the muse—that is, acquiring the creativity habit—don't try to lose weight or quit smoking or take up running at the same time. Give yourself two weeks to six months to establish your connection with the muse before devoting attention to other habits.

3. **KEEP IT POSITIVE.** The subconscious mind cannot process negation, so be sure that when you sweet-talk your muse, you use positive statements: "I am an imaginative writer," (rather than "I am not a boring writer").

I have a dear friend named John whom I've known for nearly thirty years. We were reporters for a business paper back in the early days of our writing careers. I gave him his first job in editorial. I didn't want to hire him. He wasn't a writer; he worked in what was then known as the paste-up department, laying out the ads for the paper. My boss made me hire him; he liked John. I didn't—and not only because he wasn't a skilled writer. He was a green cub reporter, and I was a first-time editor. Neither of us knew what we were doing. He fought me on every edit, was always late with his stories, annoyed the art director at every turn, and never failed to bring out the worst in me. When he challenged me, I was as likely to respond with a raspberry as I was with a civilized remark. (My managerial skills did improve eventually, but not in time for John, my first direct report.)

John's background was in painting. He'd studied art at the University of Iowa before coming to California. I didn't know him then, but I'd seen the photos of him—a wild-haired, bearded artist in paint-splattered overalls wielding a brush like a torch—and I'd seen his work—bold, uninhibited, even violent images spilled on the canvas like so much blood. But he seemed to have lost that freedom of expression when he switched from the canvas to the page. He got better at writing, but he tortured himself in the process. He would call me on the phone, having missed another deadline, and say, "I am writhing on the floor in agony." I would laugh, as he wanted me to do (my laughter granted him another several hours), but I knew that he was dead serious.

John continued to write, and he continued to torture himself. He got better; in fact, he got great. A full-time freelance writer for many years now, he specializes in high-tech reportage and has penned countless articles and columns as well as several nonfiction books. But at heart he's a fiction writer—one of the most talented storytellers I know. The only problem? He can't seem to finish any fiction. He wants to—it is his secret life's wish—but he can't. Which makes me crazy, because I know I could sell it. More important, I know he could be one of the greats—Stephen King great, Ray Bradbury great, Neil Gaiman great.

But to do that, he'd have to find the fun in it—just as he found the fun in painting as a young man. Enough fun to silence his self-torment.

If you are waiting for a happy ending to this story, there isn't one. At least not yet. But with any luck, John will learn to play again—to write with quiet hands—and readers, myself included, will rejoice.

INSPIRATION ON DEMAND

"Serious art is born of serious play."
—JULIA CAMERON

When I think of a writer at play, I think of Ray Bradbury. I met him once, early in my career, at the Santa Barbara Writers Conference. It was my first real writers conference, and going was a declaration of independence. My friend Susan and I made the trip in her Volvo station wagon, two writers masquerading as suburban homemakers. Susan had quit her job as a reporter for Fairchild Fashion Media when she'd married and had kids. We met at the local park and fell into each other's company like veterans of a foreign war. We'd spent nearly a year plotting our week-long escape to Santa Barbara. Our expectations were nothing if not high.

Ray Bradbury met those expectations—and more. Bradbury was the Dalai Lama of writers, an enlightened storyteller almost childlike in his enthusiasm for his craft. His joy was contagious; he made you feel good about being a writer and challenged you to enjoy the actual process of writing as much as he did. As he told us—and I took it to heart—"the first thing a writer should be is *excited.*"

DRILL IT DOWN

Think of the last time you read a story in which it was obvious that the writer had a ball writing it. Reread that book, and ask yourself why you think she had such fun. How does her enthusiasm translate to the page? What about the language, the style, the plot, and/or the characters leads you to believe this? Moreover, why did you have so much fun reading it? What have you learned that you can apply to your own writing process?

If you need reminding what excitement looks like, spend some time with children. Any child at play will do, but small children are best—they have not yet had excitement shamed out of them. Think of toddlers digging for wiggling worms in the backyard, kindergartners set loose with finger paints and rolls of blank paper, school-age kids in the sun on the beach building castles and forts out of sand and sea. Even teenagers—out of the grown-ups' earshot—will drop the adolescent masks of apathy when texting or rapping or hanging out playing video games.

As a writer, it is your mission to recapture that childlike enthusiasm for play. This capacity for play is also a capacity for joy. I'm not saying that every word you write has to be a fun and happy experience—just a playful experience, the mere prospect of which excites you.

Excitement is often made up of equal parts anxiety, anticipation, and, ultimately, exhilaration. Watch a toddler learn to walk: the fearful first steps into the void, the frustration of the inevitable fall, the overwhelming determination to succeed, and, at long last, the unparalleled delight in the final wobbling that marks victory.

The toddler's path is the path of every creative person. The trick is to rekindle the excitement that fuels the toddler in your writer's soul. For toddlers, learning to walk is a game they must win. Sure, they could continue to crawl—the safer and more reliable form of travel—but one by one, they pull themselves up and master the art of walking. And then, much to their parents' trepidation, they win the ultimate boon: They run!

Life for a toddler is one exciting moment after another—serious play that reaps serious rewards. When I was a child, I spent a lot of time with the neighborhood kids playing war. (Before you judge us too harshly, do remember that my neighborhood was an armed camp, as I spent most of my childhood on Army bases, where war was the dominant metaphor of our young lives. We played war the way other kids played hide-and-seek and kick the can.)

I was a good soldier. But, cursed with a short attention span, I would often grow tired of war games and try to convince my pals to play school instead. Of course, I always insisted on being the teacher, which may have explained their reluctance to play along. I liked being the boss, running playtime for me and my playmates—and my commanding play proved good preparation for the writing life.

For when you're writing, you're playing, but you're in *command* of that play. If you're writing a thriller, the game could be a suspenseful, terrifying game of cat and mouse. If you're writing a romance, the game of love could be a dark, tragic tale of unrequited passion—or a boy-meets-girl fable with a meet-cute and a happy ending worthy of Nora Ephron. If you're writing a family drama, the game could be a domestic war that makes *Who's Afraid of Virginia Woolf?* look like child's play.

Television and movies draw directly from the games children play without apology or attribution:

- For every kid who's played hide-and-seek after dark or dared a pal to spend a long and spooky night in the local cemetery, there's a horror film based on the same premise.
- For every little girl who's played out domestic dramas with Barbie and Ken and Midge and Skipper—in which dolls pretend to be girls who make pretend pancakes in pretend kitchens for pretend babies only to end up having pretend affairs and getting pretend divorces—there's a Doris Day and Rock Hudson movie or a *Sex and the City* episode or a series like Lena Dunham's *Girls*.
- For every boy who's hung out with his friends, teasing one another and challenging one another to do stupid things, there's a slapstick comedy featuring the Marx Brothers or the Three Stooges or the guys from *The Hangover* franchise. (I never liked, nor did I understand, these stories until I had sons of my own. My oldest boy proved incapable of refusing any dare issued by another boy. Suffice it to say that we spent a lot of time in the emergency room and the principal's office because he was always in trouble for such stunts as jumping off the roofs of buildings and joyriding in school vehicles because a friend as clueless as he was would dare him to do it. Boys being stupid—that's the basic plot for every bro-mance ever written.)

How have your favorite childhood games—playing with miniature plastic pots and pans, dinosaurs, or action figures; tossing around baseballs or footballs or basketballs with your teammates; dressing up in your mom's nightgowns, costume jewelry, and high heels—influenced your choice of genre today? Are you sure that you are playing in the right genre?

The Play's the Thing

Speaking of play, there's a reason that even dramas as serious as the aforementioned Edward Albee masterpiece *Who's Afraid of Virginia Woolf?* are called plays. Think about it: In the theater, plays are comprised of words and actions written by one person and performed on a stage by actors portraying imaginary men and women doing imaginary things in imaginary places in order to entertain the audience. As a storyteller, you do the same thing—only you do it without the benefit of the stage or the actors or the audience. You sit alone in a room making up imaginary people doing imaginary things in imaginary places. That's playing—whether you enjoy the process or not. So you may as well take a cue from our friend Ray Bradbury and enjoy the hell out of it.

"Inspiration Meets Craft" Equals "Practice Meets Play"

Having fun when you write means rediscovering your sense of play. Look to the games you loved as a child—especially the ones you played when left on your own—for clues on how to develop a playful attitude toward your work.

As an only child, I spent a lot of time alone. Especially in the summer, when we typically moved to a new place—with no school in session and many kids on vacation, I was forced to amuse myself. So I went on a lot of long walks in the woods with my little poodle Rogue, climbed a lot of apple trees, ate a lot of sour apples, and read a lot of books high in the branches, my faithful dog in wait below. I've replicated this playtime in my adult writing life. As long as I have apples, books, and a dog by my side, I can usually settle down to write quite happily. When the muse eludes me, I take a long walk in the woods.

Your sense of play is critical to establishing and maintaining a regular writing practice. In order to master your craft, you have to work at it day after day, week after week, month after month, year after year. The paradox here is simply this: To do something well, you have to like doing it enough to devote enough time to do it well—and yet to like doing something, you have to do it well enough to like doing it. Most of us like doing things we're good at—and eventually we stop doing things we feel we're not very good at.

Play and practice go hand in hand, just like inspiration and craft. Or at least they should. Dorothy Parker famously said that she hated writing but loved having written—and many writers have joined that chorus since. But let's remember that she drank to excess.

Better to be one of those writers who loves the writing process—and can't get enough of it. When it comes to role models, you're better off choosing Ray Bradbury over Dorothy Parker any day.

And before we move on to how to establish a solid writing practice, let's give him the last word: "You must stay drunk on writing so reality cannot destroy you."

HANDS ON

Remember your favorite games as a child—and play them again. (If you need other people to play them with you, recruit your kids or grandkids. If you don't have kids or grandkids, borrow some.) What about these play experiences might summon your muse? How might you incorporate these games into your writing practice?

CHAPTER THREE

writing as practice

"Anything we fully do is an alone journey."
—NATALIE GOLDBERG

Now that you know how to engage your muse, it's time to marry craft and inspiration and put it on the page. This is the part where you actually have to write something. Where you sit down and write word after word for hours a day every day until you reach The End. This is otherwise known as practice.

The word *practice* gets a bad rep. It reminds us of all those painful hours we spent practicing the piano as a kid. Or at least that's what it reminds me of: suffering under the tutelage of Sister Elizabeth at St. Peter and Paul's Elementary School in Cincinnati, Ohio. Sister Elizabeth was not one of those lovely singing nuns from *The Sound of Music*. She was old and mean and scary looking and wielded her brown wooden ruler like a kendo master. I was seven years old when my parents got a piano and signed me up for lessons. Neither of them played the piano, and I don't remember wanting to play—at the time I was all about my new bicycle—but nonetheless all good 1960s parents got their kids piano lessons, and my parents were nothing if not perfect 1960s parents.

I was supposed to practice playing the piano an hour a day, with my little hands curved in the shape of what Sister Elizabeth called pigpens. I had no idea what she was talking about; I'd never seen a pigpen before. All I knew about pigs was from the story *The Three Little Pigs*, and they lived in houses made of straw and wood and brick, none of which featured curves. Sister Elizabeth's image of a pigpen did not resonate with me; even at the tender age of seven I already trusted stories more than I trusted grown-ups.

Those who attended Catholic schools can guess what happened next. Whenever my fingers failed to curl into this proscribed pigpen-style arch, out came the ruler. Sister Elizabeth would smack my hands, hard, time and time again, over the course of every lesson. To add insult to injury—the default mode of wicked teachers everywhere—a very displeased Sister Elizabeth called my parents in for a special teacher/parent conference, in which she informed them that Paula Sue's progress at the piano was unsatisfactory. Not because I couldn't transform my fingers into pigpens but—horror of horrors—because my parents had failed to exert the proper discipline on their *only* child. They had failed to make me *practice*.

My parents were mortified. Especially my father, who was a captain at the time, teaching ROTC at Xavier University.

It was bad enough for a good Catholic to be called on the carpet by a nun for being a subpar parent, but for a captain in the U.S. Army to be reprimanded by a civilian over disciplining his child—well, that was simply unacceptable.

My punishment was twofold: (1) two lessons a week instead of one with the triumphant Sister Elizabeth, and (2) practice, practice, and more practice, supervised on good days by my compassionate mother and on bad days by my far more rigorous father.

I hated Sister Elizabeth, I hated the piano, and, most of all, I hated practice. My reprieve came as it always did: We moved. (This is the glorious part of moving, the part no one ever talks about. If you hate a place, or its people, or just who you are while you're there, moving is a get-out-of-jail-free card that grants you a new start.) My dad went to Korea, and Mom and I went to Oklahoma to live until he returned a year later. The piano went into the garage. Sometimes, when no one was looking, I would sneak in and play it, just for fun.

That was practice, too, but it wasn't fun enough to keep me coming back often enough to make a difference. I still can't play the piano, and the truth is, I don't much care. What I did practice as a child was reading:

I read all the time, I grew to be a very good reader, and now I make a living reading. Of course, I also practiced ballet and tap dancing and the guitar and cooking, and while I'm no dancer or musician or chef, I still use those skills in my adult life from time to time.

If you hate the word *practice*, you probably have a Sister Elizabeth in your past as well. But you must have liked something well enough as a child to practice it, whether you called it that or not. What you liked to practice when you were a kid—the flute or free throws, computers or crochet—can inform your writing practice today.

A QUESTION OF CRAFT

What did you practice enough to learn to do it well? When and where did you practice? Did you practice alone or in a group? What did you like about it? What motivations drove you? What satisfactions did it provide? What rituals accompanied the practice? The answers to these questions hold the secrets to establishing a writing routine you can live by today.

SHOWING UP

"Exercise the writing muscle every day, even if it is only a letter, notes, a title list, a character sketch, a journal entry. Writers are like dancers, like athletes. Without that exercise, the muscles seize up."
—JANE YOLEN

Woody Allen once said that 90 percent of success is showing up. Allen practices what he preaches: He's been showing up at his typewriter—the very same 1950s-era manual Olympia portable SM-3—for the past fifty years, producing a breathtaking oeuvre of jokes, cartoons, plays, monologues, essays, short stories, and, of course, scripts. When he finishes one piece, he slips another piece of paper into the typewriter.

Life comes with millions of built-in distractions. Some of these distractions—making a living and working out and raising kids and running a household—may be nonnegotiable. Others—television and hobbies and social media—may be up for examination. But whatever the distractions that clutter your day, you can declutter your time and carve out a clean, spare space in which to write.

This time is critical. Most successful writers have a regular writing schedule, and they keep to it. Most write every day. Annie Dillard writes in the mornings and then goes out to lunch. John Updike wrote every weekday and took weekends off. Maya Angelou rented a hotel room in her hometown and checked herself in from 6:30 A.M. to 2 P.M. to write every day.

Showing up every day to write is one of the rules you break at your peril. And yet it's one that many writers take a long time to learn, myself included. When my kids were little, I wrote during their naps and after they went to bed, but once I got my first nine-to-five job as a reporter, I found it much harder to make the time to work on my fiction. And it wasn't just because I was too busy.

This was partly because the creative impulse—the itch we creative people need to scratch on a daily basis to stay sane—was often satisfied by the demands of writing and editing stories for the paper. I had always counted on that compulsion to get me to the blank page, but by the time I got home from work, I'd already filled tons of blank pages. My creative self was spent.

Another factor affected my ability to find time for my novel as well. As a journalist, you're a working writer. You don't need inspiration to show up; it's your job to show up. You write what you're told to write; your editor and the news itself dictate what you write and when you write it. You write a specified number of inches for the paper about a given topic, and you do it fast. There's no time for writer's block; there's no time to panic or procrastinate. Your deadline is a hard stop; if you miss your deadline, your story doesn't appear in the paper—and you are out of a job.

As a gainfully employed reporter, my parameters were very clear—and I worked well within them. But when left on my own as a freelance fiction writer, I faltered. No deadline? No output. Without the pressure of a hard stop, I rarely even started. I consoled—and excused—myself by telling anyone who would listen that being a single working mom who wrote all day and cared for the kids all night made it impossible for me to do anything else. I felt very virtuous and very sorry for myself.

Until I met Rob. Rob was hired on at the same business publication where I worked, and we commuted together to the office forty miles each way from Santa Cruz to Monterey. It was two hours a day stuck in a car with a writer who bettered me in every way. Rob was already a published author; his first novel had been published by a small literary press in San Francisco. I read it and admittedly only understood enough of it to know that I was sharing my commute with a guy way smarter and more productive than I.

Rob came from the "no excuses" school of writing. Forget deadlines and creative impulses and kids and jobs and everything else. Writers write.

When I told him my writer's sob story, he told me that he got up every morning at 4 A.M. to write. By the time he picked me up, he'd already put in two hours of writing fiction. *Morning person,* I thought, cursing my own late-night biorhythms.

But as it turned out, I couldn't chalk up the fact that he wrote fiction every day and I did not to his being blessed with the circadian rhythms of a rooster. Rob wrote when he could. He couldn't write during the day because he was at the office. He couldn't write at night because he was watching his two-year-old daughter and six-month-old twins (!) while his wife worked the late shift. So he wrote before the sun came up. Every morning. Rain or shine or teething.

Rob taught me that *writers write,* come what may. I learned that if I wasn't writing fiction, that was okay—at this point I was the only one who *needed* me to write my novel—but that I had no one to blame but myself.

The same is true for you. If you want to be a writer, don't leave your writing to chance. Schedule time to write into your daily life— and then show up.

WRITE IT DOWN

Get a pen and some paper, and set a timer for fifteen minutes. Write down what you did yesterday, from the minute you opened your eyes to the last moments before you nodded off to sleep. Be as detailed as possible, and include a time line:

- 6 A.M.: shower and dress
- 6:30 A.M.: breakfast, reading the paper, cleaning up
- 7 A.M.: walk the dog
- 7:30 A.M.: leave for work

You get the idea. When you're finished, take a hard look at the way you spend your time—and where you could squeeze in more time to write.

TAKING YOUR SEAT

"The scariest moment is always just before you start."
—STEPHEN KING

Okay, so you've carved out the time to write. You're setting your alarm an hour earlier every morning, or you've given up *The Big Bang Theory* reruns, or you're staying up after your family has gone to bed to write because, as Elizabeth Jolley says, "I am not needed in their dreams."

You've got the time. Now what? Now you sit down and write.

This is where the trouble often starts. You sit down at your dining room table, whose surface now holds only your computer, ready to write. Then you get up because your butt hurts and you'd forgotten how uncomfortable your dining room chairs are and you couldn't possibly sit here and create for any length of time. Or you sit down on your couch, cross-legged, your laptop balanced on your knees, ready to write. Then you get up because your stomach growls and you realize that you're hungry and you know the synapses in your brain won't fire properly without sufficient protein. Or you sit at your desk during your office's official lunch hour, door closed, ready to write. Then you get up because your colleague knocks on the door to remind you that it's the boss's birthday and everyone's taking her out to lunch, and while you could miss it, you are up for that promotion and as you're not successful enough as a writer quite yet to quit your day job, you'd better make nice and go.

Another day's writing avoided.

Taking your seat—even when you've made the time—can prove more difficult than you anticipated. But it's usually simply getting started that is tough. We aren't talking about a true writer's block here; we'll go into that later in chapter thirteen. We're talking the low-grade unease that hits us whenever we sit down to write, the performance anxiety that afflicts all performers, from surgeons to actors.

More than 80 percent of professional actors admit to suffering stage fright at least once during their careers, according to a study by Fielding Graduate University. Surgeons rarely admit to anything resembling fear, but Dr. Charlie Brown, an expert in performance psychology, says that it's "not uncommon for surgeons and physicians to use beta-blockers to treat symptoms of anxiety associated with performance."

Actors face public humiliation when they set foot on the stage; surgeons face life and death itself when they step into the operating theater. Yet the show—and the operation—must go on. We do our writing alone, and the only lives at stake are those of imaginary people. But there's something we can learn from actors and surgeons—and that something has to do with ritual.

Ritual can help you get through those first lines, those first cuts, those first words. The *physical, mental,* and *emotional* aspects of ritual prepare you to launch into your performance.

Place is the *physical* aspect of ritual. The actor has the theater; merely treading the boards invites the spotlight. The surgeon has the operating theater; he presides over the operating table in a performance that can mean the life or death of his patient. For writers, where we write is important, in that it needs to be a place that we associate with writing, a space consecrated to our art. Writing is a sacred act—and so you must create a sacred space in which to do it. Dedicate a studio, a spare room, even a corner of your den to your work—and equip it with the tools and talismans that will inspire you to write every day. If you can't—or won't—

work at home, then try the west wing of your local library or the corner table by the window in your favorite coffee shop.

Regalia comprise the *mental* aspect of ritual. These are the trappings that allow you to get into character and prepare for your performance. The actor applies makeup and dons a costume and warms up her voice and body. The surgeon reviews the X-rays and MRIs and CAT scans, puts on his scrubs, and washes his hands and arms for a full five minutes, during which time he visualizes the procedure he is about to perform. For writers, regalia may take the form of pajamas or sweatpants or a suit and tie, a review of the previous day's work, a pot of tea or a can of soda or a bottle of water, twenty minutes of meditation or a three-mile run—whatever helps you assert the writer in you.

Tools represent the *emotional* aspect of ritual. These are the weapons you bring to the fight, the talismans that give you the courage to act once the battle cry goes up. For the actor, the overture plays, the curtain rises, the audience quiets, and she steps into the spotlight and breaks the hush with her first line. The surgeon enters the operating theater, consults with his colleagues, inspects his sterile instruments, checks the patient on the table, chooses a scalpel, and, accompanied by the music of his choice (or silence) and under the glare of the surgical lights, he makes the first cut. For writers, the tools of the trade that ease the transition from blank page to work in progress are a matter of personal taste and productivity. Write on paper or tablets, with pen or pencil or stylus, with music on or television off—whatever allows you to make that first mark.

THE SURGEON'S PLAYLIST

Music accompanies surgeons at the operating table more often than not, according to the *British Medical Journal.* Classical music is most common and is lauded by operating room staff for its role in "reducing stress and improving communication."

But which kind of music improves performance is in the ear of the listener: Some studies indicate that classical music is better than heavy metal or hard rock, but others reveal that reggae and hip-hop most benefit a surgeon's performance.

One piece that anyone who might have to administer CPR can agree on is "Stayin' Alive" by the Bee Gees, a song whose beat mimics the correct compression rate needed for CPR should the patient go into cardiac arrest.

You might consider adding that song to your playlist so that you're prepared the next time you think the stress of being a writer might give you a heart attack.

"When you sit down to practice, however casually, you cast yourself as a hero and victim of your own myth; you will encounter obstacles, you will struggle, succeed, and struggle some more." —GLENN KURTZ

DRILL IT DOWN

Ritual is the hallmark of any established practice. How do you practice writing? How might you ritualize this process? Think of a recent writing session in which you were most pleased by the quality and/or quantity of your work. What about the place, regalia, and tools characterized that session and contributed to your productivity? What sabotaged it? How might you adjust your ritual to facilitate your best work?

The Yoga of Writing

"I used to be a pre-industrial writer: thousands of words in a spurt and then a few days off. But as I get older, I've switched to a mode best described as 'slow and steady wins the race.' Basically, I write during the same four hours every day, after breakfast and the all-important coffee, generally in the same room and wearing the same pajamas." —SCOTT WESTERFELD

Like Scott Westerfeld, I, too, wrote in spurts for many years. The reasons for this were many. First and foremost, most of the books I've published have been written under contract, which means they were written under deadlines. Because I began my career as a reporter, I've always been very deadline driven—give me a contracted deadline, and I write to that deadline. I produced these books on my own time, outside of my day job, so I wrote mostly on the weekends when I could set aside several hours in which to write one or more chapters at a time. I didn't have a daily writing practice because I wasn't writing for practice; I was writing to publish, and I had a deadline set by a publishing schedule.

That was my excuse. And it worked—at least for contracted projects. But my most important work, the novels I had to write in their entirety without benefit of contract *before* I could find a publisher, remained unfinished. Writing on spec forced me to establish artificial deadlines— deadlines I never took seriously. Without a writing practice, I started and abandoned several novels—and actually finished only the books I was contracted to write.

And then I took up yoga. I didn't mean to; after nearly two decades in California I thought of yogis as touchy-feely, woo-woo Type Bs who spent too much time in hot tubs. I lumped writers who did yoga into that same category. But after another year of not finishing a novel, I treated myself to a Julia Cameron writers workshop with the hope of discovering what I was doing wrong.

Julia Cameron, author of the classic *The Artist's Way* and one of the most influential writing teachers of our time, was coming to Kripalu, the yoga and wellness center in the Berkshires, only a 150-mile drive from my home. I'd taken one of her creativity workshops twenty years before, and I had loved it. I thought if anyone could help me get my writer's juice back, it was Julia Cameron.

I talked my writer friend Susan into going with me to Kripalu, worried that I'd feel uncomfortable in a room full of yogis twisting into pretzels and eating sprouts and saying "Namaste" all the time. But to my surprise I felt immediately at home at Kripalu, partly because the setting's look and feel reflected its origins as a Jesuit seminary and partly because the people seemed so welcoming and, well, so enlightened. Julia

Cameron was as wonderfully inspiring as I remembered her, and Susan and I both loved her workshop.

Like all of the workshops at Kripalu, it was designed to provide time for contemplation and yoga as well as writing and learning. Always one to get the most for my money, I took a yoga class—and fell in love. When I came home, I was determined not only to finish a novel but to find a yoga class like the one I had just attended. One of my Mystery Writers of America pals pointed me to a local studio run by a Kripalu-trained yoga teacher, and I signed up. Within a year I was hooked and so dedicated to my yoga practice that I enrolled in yoga teacher training. Now I'm a certified instructor, but more important, I'm a yoga practitioner. I've learned the art of daily practice—and I've applied it to my writing life as well.

Yoga taught me that what's important is coming to the mat, whether you feel like it or not. I know that if I just come to my mat every day, I may accomplish things I'd never have dreamed possible. Like learning to stand on my head for the first time in my life at age fifty-four. Like sitting still in a full lotus position to quiet my monkey mind long enough to meditate. Like finally establishing a regular writing practice that doesn't depend on deadlines or contracts but on the deep desires of my true writer's soul.

This is what writing as practice can do for you, too. Taking your seat—like coming to your mat—will, over time, help you delve deeper and deeper into your writing practice, deeper and deeper into your writing.

In some ways, writing is like learning to drive. When you first get behind the wheel, you're thrilled and scared and overly conscious of every detail: the pressure of your foot on the gas pedal and then the brake as you navigate stop-and-go traffic, the anticipation you feel when you realize that the light ahead of you is changing to yellow just as you approach a busy intersection, the vehicles you can see in the rearview mirror that you're supposed to check every five to eight seconds. Every minute on the road seems like an hour; you (and your instructor) breathe more easily when the lesson is over. (I'll never forget how my driving instructor in Ft. Leavenworth screamed when I nearly sideswiped a military police car during one of my first lessons.)

writing with quiet hands

Driving is such a stressful and demanding activity that more than half of all people fail their first driving test—and new drivers have higher crash rates than experienced drivers, no matter what their age. And yet, once we master the basics of driving, our odds of having an accident drop, along with our anxiety level. Soon, as a result of our practice, driving becomes second nature; we grow so comfortable that we don't think twice about getting in the car and driving away, regardless of traffic or weather or destination. We just drive.

Writing practice yields the same results. Take your seat every day, and pretty soon you won't think twice about getting into your story and getting words on the page. You'll just write.

THE GOOD, THE BAD, AND THE UGLY DAYS

"If you have a limited amount of time to write, you just sit down and do it. You might not write well every day, but you can always edit a page. You can't edit a blank page." —JODI PICOULT

Establishing a writing practice means taking your seat every day with the faith that if you sit long enough, the words will come. But sometimes you sit down, ready to write through the butt aches and the hunger and the lure of a good restaurant lunch ... and nothing happens. Not a word comes to mind, much less to the blank page.

You are tempted to throw in the towel and go to the movies. *It's just one day,* you think. And you'd be right. But don't abandon your seat quite yet. There are several techniques you can use to get the words going again.

- **THE HOURGLASS.** One of my favorite gifts for new writers is an hourglass. Using an hourglass is an easy way to get into the flow of writing when you find yourself resisting your practice. Most "hourglasses" are sand timers that count out different segments of time, from two minutes to a full hour; I find that fifteen-minute sand timers are the best. Just tell yourself you only have to write for fifteen minutes, and turn over your hourglass. Write anything—even if it's just "I hate writing, and I hate hourglasses, and I hate you"—and keep writing until the sands have all slipped away. Nine times out of ten you won't even notice because you'll be in the flow.

- **IF ... THEN.** If you're thinking that this is a time-honored plotting technique—"*If* my protagonist does X, *then* Y will happen"—well, you're half right. But *If ... then* statements are also a great way to reward yourself for taking your seat every day. *If ... then* statements resonate with your subconscious, so keep them simple: "*If* I write the scene in which my heroine meets her love interest for the first time, *then* I can read the next chapter of *Gone Girl* before I go to bed."

- **SET A WORD-COUNT GOAL.** Some writers prefer setting a word-count goal for writing practice rather than specifying a given time frame. If this works for you, great—just don't set the goal so high that you struggle to meet it or so low that meeting it is too easy. Experiment with various counts to see which daily target works best for you. *Note:* Setting word-count goals can be particularly effective when you have a hard-stop deadline to meet.

- **PLAY A MOVIE IN YOUR MIND.** Your subconscious responds to images, which is why you can use visualization to jump-start your writing whenever you feel stalled. Close your eyes, and watch your story unfold. Picture the next scene you need to write—the one where the killer traps the hero in that burning building—and watch what happens, frame by frame. Now open your eyes, and write it down.

- **DON'T JUDGE; JUST WRITE.** Don't think about whether the words you are thinking about writing down are any good; just write them down. When you are tempted to quit your practice today because you think your work is, well, crap, just keep writing. When you review your words tomorrow, odds are they will be just fine. We are never the best judges of our work, *especially* while we are writing it.

- **YOU/I AFFIRMATIONS.** When all else fails, simply create an affirmation that addresses your angst, and repeat it until you can settle down to write. Here's one that some of my clients (who worry too much about whether they are going to sell their work) have found effective: *I am a gifted writer, and I can write anything I want.*

Practice long enough, and sooner or later the rituals you put into place will train you to write on command. Just like Pavlov's dogs, you'll come running to take your seat whenever you hear the bell.

All you have to do is ring it.

Sleep, Creep, Leap

"A book is a garden ... ." —Charles Baudelaire

There's an old adage in gardening: Sleep, creep, leap. This typically refers to the growth pattern of newly planted perennials, provided they are nourished with sun and water and nutrients: The first year the plant will "sleep," the second year the plant will "creep," and the third year the plant will "leap."

As your writing practice deepens over time, you will grow as a writer—in much the same way as a well-nourished perennial. You'll take your seat, and you'll write. You may think you are getting nowhere, but as you keep at it, and your pages pile up, you are literally growing yourself as a writer.

At first, this development may be unnoticeable—that's the sleep part. But before you know it, you'll find your prose creeping along toward good and then leaping right into great. Growth rates vary for writers just as they vary for plants, but whether your "sleep, creep, leap" development takes three months, three years, or three decades will depend on what you learn as you explore the many places your practice may take you and how quickly you apply that knowledge to your work in progress.

In the next chapter, we'll take a look at one of the most important ways in which your practice can help you enrich your work: voice.

HANDS ON, PART ONE

Just as you broke down your day in the previous exercise, break down your writing practice. Enumerate all the rituals you have investigated in this chapter, and brainstorm new ways in which you might enhance your writing practice. Create a new plan for

---

your writing practice that incorporates what works best for you. Mine might look something like this:

- 6 A.M. to 8 A.M.: make coffee, walk the dog, read
- 8 A.M. to 12 P.M.: day job
- Lunchtime: yoga/meditation
- 1 P.M. to 6 P.M.: day job
- 6 P.M. to 7:45 P.M.: prepare and enjoy dinner with my family
- 7:45 P.M.: make a pot of tea, and read yesterday's work while I drink my chai and indulge in some chocolate
- 8 P.M. to 10 P.M.: write on my laptop in my pajamas, cross-legged on my couch, with *PBS* on the television in the background
- 10 P.M. to 10:30 P.M.: tally the word count for the day (if on deadline); brainstorm ideas and make notes for tomorrow's writing in my sketchbook
- 10:30 P.M.: read until I fall asleep

I know that reading, walking, cooking, yoga, and meditation all feed my writing practice. So does brainstorming in my sketchbook. Most important of all: coffee, tea, and chocolate!

HANDS ON, PART TWO

Now create a wish list for your practice that you can implement over time. Here's what's on my wish list: a standing desk to help me maintain a sound posture while I write, a handwriting app and a new stylus for my iPad so I can capture my nocturnal scribbling, a blue cashmere robe to wear as I write on the coldest days of winter.

Remember that your writing practice should grow and change as you do. What works for you for one season or for one project may not work for the next. Staying alert to signs of growth—and adapting as necessary—will keep your writing practice alive and take you where you want to go as a writer.

CHAPTER FOUR

a voice of your own

"Your writing voice is the deepest possible reflection of who you are. The job of your voice is not to seduce or flatter or make well-shaped sentences. In your voice, your readers should be able to hear the contents of your mind, your heart, your soul." —MEG ROSOFF

Voice is who you are as a storyteller: your language, your syntax, and your diction for sure, but, more important, your truth. Finding your voice is as simple—and as difficult—as finding your truth.

Readers recognize that truth when they see it—and they seek it out. Readers, agents and editors and reviewers among them, are suckers for a strong voice. When readers fall in love with a writer's voice, they will follow it, line after line, page after page, and book after book.

As a reader, I prefer writers with a strong voice; as a writer, I look for voice lessons from writers known for their voices. And as an agent, I search for writers with a distinct voice—because I know that voice alone can sell a story.

Discovering your voice—your true north—may be what makes readers fall in love with you, too. Think of *The Catcher in the Rye* by J.D. Salinger. Millions of readers fell in love with Salinger's voice when they read his classic novel of adolescent male angst, not just because his voice was funny and compelling but because it rang true. (I should note that when I first read the book when I was a young girl, I never finished it. It didn't ring true for me at all. Twenty-five years later, my teenage son had to read the novel for school, which meant that I had to read it again to help him with his book report. This time I read the story all the way through with great pleasure. The voice rang true for me and engaged me thoroughly, because as the mother of an adolescent male, I could finally see the truth in it.)

Tell a story in your own strong and authentic voice, and you may win readers based on the voice alone. Tell a *great* story in your own strong and authentic voice, and you may win the kind of readership these writers have:

> My father's family name being Pirrip, and my Christian name Philip, my infant tongue could make of both names nothing longer or more explicit than Pip. So, I called myself Pip, and came to be called Pip.
> —Charles Dickens, *Great Expectations*

> 124 was spiteful. Full of a baby's venom. The women in the house knew it and so did the children.
>
> —Toni Morrison, *Beloved*

> The terror, which would not end for another twenty-eight years—if it ever did—began, so far as I know or can tell, with a boat made from a sheet of newspaper floating down the gutter swollen with rain.
> —Stephen King, *It*

> It is a truth universally acknowledged, that a single man in possession of a good fortune, must be in want of a wife.
>
> However little known the feelings or views of such a man may be on his first entering the neighbourhood, this truth is so well fixed in the minds of the surrounding families, that he is considered as the rightful property of some one or other of their daughters.
> —Jane Austen, *Pride and Prejudice*

> The night Max wore his wolf suit and made mischief of one kind and another his mother called him "WILD THING!" and Max said "I'LL EAT YOU UP!" so he was sent to bed without eating anything.
> —Maurice Sendak, *Where the Wild Things Are*

These are all writers with strong, unique voices that continue to engage, entertain, and enlighten readers over the test of time. Each tells the truth of life as the writer knows it:

- Dickens crusades for a better life for the underprivileged in Victorian England—and his truth emboldens change.
- Morrison shines a bright light on the realities of racism, identity, and community in a voice that is part herald, part destroyer, and part shaman.
- King brings the truth of our very nightmares to light in a voice all the more terrifying for its commonness.
- Austen tells the truth about men and women in a time when women were often defined by their relationships with men, like it or not.
- Sendak reveals the truth about the mysteries and miseries of childhood in a voice as mischievous and magical as children themselves.

Achieving that voice—the authentic expression of your unique truth that you use to engage, entertain, and enlighten your own readers—is one of the biggest challenges you face as a writer. Some writers do it naturally, but most of us have to dig for it. It's a discovery process that will not only inform your writing, but your life as well.

Note: This chapter is full of invitations to write. Accept those invitations, even when you are tempted to skip them.

A QUESTION OF CRAFT

Imagine your mother's voice. Often this is the first voice you know, the one you learn to recognize in the womb, the voice that most affects you, for better or worse, once you enter the world. Now imagine you've had a bad day. Your spouse left you; your boss fired you; your dog died. You tell your mother. What would your mother say to you? How would she say it? Write it down, or record it on your phone. Now read it aloud or play it back on your phone. What language, syntax, diction, and tone characterize that well-known voice?

Now imagine the same scenario—only you're the mother talking to your adult child after a bad day. What would you

CREATIVE IMITATION

"Originality is nothing but judicious imitation. The most original writers borrowed from one another. The instruction we find in books is like fire. We fetch it from our neighbors, kindle it at home, communicate it to others, and it becomes the property of all." —VOLTAIRE

When we first start to write, many of us imitate those writers whose work we most admire and/or have read most widely. This is fine; such imitation can be instructive in more ways than one. Not only can you learn the ins and outs of writing in a given authorial style, you can learn what to co-opt in developing your own voice.

I've mentioned my admiration of Alice Hoffman. I own first editions of all her work, attend her readings whenever I can, and have half a novel written in an unabashedly faux Alice Hoffman voice. But attempting to write that novel helped me expand the horizons of my own voice and taught me how to tell stories in a more meaningful way, and to take risks that I would not normally have taken.

Ask yourself which writers you most admire, whose voices you are most apt to adopt, other than your own, when writing. Now ask yourself what appeals to you about their writing and what you can incorporate into your own work.

Early in her career, best-selling thriller writer Hank Phillippi Ryan was advised to consider the question "Who do you want to be?" That is, whose career did she want to emulate? This question can be related to voice as well. The trick is to discover which aspects are organic to your own work and which are not. Which are yours to steal—and which are not?

Writer, Know Thyself

Knowing yourself—and accepting your strengths and weaknesses, possibilities and limitations—is critical to identifying and developing a distinctive voice. Describe yourself, on a separate sheet of paper, in the first ten words that come to mind.

Now, contact your best friend, and have her or him describe you in ten words. Which words are the same? Which are different? Make a master list that combines both lists, and then match up those qualities at random with your favorite writers, the ones you'd like to be when you grow up.

For example, my list might look like this:

funny	Alice Hoffman
gregarious	Jane Austen
bossy	Mark Nepo
optimistic	Robert B. Parker
yogic	Anne Lamott
klutzy	Elizabeth Berg

Consider your own list. What clues to your authentic voice can be found there?

CLUES TO YOUR AUTHENTIC VOICE

Your true voice sounds like you, only better. If you're funny, it's funny; if you're passionate, it's passionate; if you're whimsical, it's whimsical.

But we all have two selves: (1) the public face, the one we show the world, and (2) the hidden face, the one we shelter from the world. Maybe your authentic voice reflects the seductress beneath a shy exterior, the mischievous child beneath the responsible adult, the outsider beneath the popular crowd-pleaser.

WALKING YOUR TALK

Part of realizing your full voice and speaking your truth is marrying what you say to how you say it. Ask yourself: What do you really want to say—and how would you like to convey that message?

Your voice can dictate how you tell your story—from pacing and plot to tone and theme. Consider the following classic stories, all about war, and all with different and distinctive voices:

- *The Things They Carried* by Tim O'Brien
- *Catch-22* by Joseph Heller
- *The People of Forever Are Not Afraid* by Shani Boianjiu
- *Gone with the Wind* by Margaret Mitchell
- *A Game of Thrones* by George R.R. Martin
- *Suite Francaise* by Irene Nemirovsky
- *War and Peace* by Leo Tolstoy
- *Slaughterhouse-Five* by Kurt Vonnegut
- *Night* by Elie Wiesel
- *The Lotus Eaters* by Tatjana Soli
- *The Kite Runner* by Khaled Hosseini
- *The Diary of a Young Girl* by Anne Frank
- *M*A*S*H** by Robert Hooker
- *The Guernsey Literary and Potato Peel Pie Society* by Mary Ann Shaffer and Annie Barrows
- *Henry VI* trilogy by William Shakespeare
- *A Long Way Gone* by Ishmael Beah

Each of these stories is shaped by the voice of the writer telling it. Choose one of the above stories; it can be one you've already read and loved or one that you haven't read before. As you read it, note how the writer's voice informs all the other elements of the story.

WRITE IT DOWN

This is a prompt that I've borrowed, with permission, from my friend, the wonderful writer Reed Farrel Coleman, best-selling, Edgar-nominated author of *Robert B. Parker's Blind Spot* (a Jesse Stone novel) and the acclaimed Moe Prager series. Reed uses this exercise whenever he teaches a class on voice.

You'll need more than one writer for this; perhaps enlist the participation of your writers' group. Invite your fellow writers to a meeting at a specific time. Let everyone get settled; pass around the wine and cheese or other refreshments. Then, about ten minutes into your time together, ask everyone in the group to write about the first ten minutes of your meeting. Allow around fifteen minutes for this timed writing. Then ask everyone to read her piece aloud. Notice the different ways in which each writer describes the same material. Note the differences in approach, language, tone, syntax, and dramatization. This exercise reveals how voice colors every writer's piece—whether the writer is aware of it or not. Learning what distinguishes your voice among all these other voices can help you refine and strengthen it going forward.

No matter what your genre, your voice should shape the story you tell. You need to reveal your truth, as best told in your own authentic voice.

If you're not sure what your truth is—or even if you think you do—you may need to dig to get to its core. Your truth is where your vein of gold lies; you need to mine it. Here's a brainstorming exercise to help you do just that. Using the following bubble chart, jot down entries for each list on a separate sheet of paper. Do this quickly—don't think about it. When you're finished, think about what comes up in this process. Which bubbles resonate with you? Which stories do you want to tell? How could they best be told in your own voice?

When a writer is telling a story to best effect, his voice rings with confidence, conviction, and creativity. Consider Salinger, whose exploration of adolescence, honesty, authenticity, and the pretense and hypocrisy of adult life are all reflected in his one-of-a-kind voice, whether he's writing about Holden Caulfield or Frannie and Zooey.

DRILL IT DOWN

You can exercise your voice just as you exercise any muscle. This means taking advantage of every opportunity to raise your voice, as in the actions below:

- Sing karaoke.
- Join your local choir.
- Keep a journal.
- Write a Letter to the Editor.
- Make a speech.
- Start a blog.

- Tell the truth about everything, big and small, for one day.
- Practice discretion.
- Practice active listening with someone you usually tune out.

HONESTY RULES

As an agent, I get very excited when I find a writer with a great voice because I know that it's easier for a writer to learn structure than to discover her truth. I often meet talented writers who have yet to sell their stories because they have yet to find their voice—or they are fighting the truth about their voice.

Part of my job is helping my clients recognize their authentic voice and tailor it to the best commercial project for them. Let me tell you four stories about four very different clients—and how they developed a distinctive voice, used that voice to tell great stories, and got published in the process. Each story offers a different voice lesson for the perceptive writer.

Reveal Yourself: A Cop's Story

When I first became an agent, I was overwhelmed by queries; my first week on the job I got more than one thousand queries from writers I didn't know from Adam, and the numbers have grown exponentially ever since. I needed an intern. (As it turns out, I always need an intern.)

I got a call from a professor friend of mine who also writes popular traditional mysteries for St. Martin's Press. She had an MFA student who was looking for an internship. She warned me that this was not your typical grad student but rather a middle-aged writer who'd spent thirty years as a homicide detective for the Oakland Police Department. I was thrilled because (1) I represented a lot of crime fiction writers who would benefit from a cop's perspective on their work, and (2) I'm a sucker for a good police procedural.

His name was Brian, and he rocked. He read my queries, he edited my clients' work, and he finished his thesis, which just so happened to be a police procedural. I liked it and offered to represent him and his work. But first he had to refine his voice.

For Brian's voice was his selling point, the leverage I needed to pitch his work when I shopped it. Cops who can write are few and far between, so when I find one, I sign him—or her—right up. But voice is a two-edged sword: Brian's experience on the force informed every word he wrote and gave his prose a confidence and authority born of that experience. All good. But not enough. What was missing in his story was how he felt about that experience. Readers would love his cop hero—but they would love him more if they got to know more about his heart—and not just his head.

This wasn't easy for Brian, who, like most cops, kept his feelings close to his bulletproof vest. I knew he thought I was making a big deal out of nothing. But he did what I asked (another reason I like working with former law-enforcement and military personnel, as they actually listen to me and follow my advice). He beefed up his protagonist's inner life, and I shopped the series. Within short order, I got Brian a three-book deal. (Look for the first in the series, *Red Line* by Brian Thiem, wherever you buy your books.)

The only real significant revision request from his editor: Beef up the inner life of his hero even *more*. (I love being right. And I love Brian.)

VOICE LESSON #1: Readers respond most to emotional honesty in a writer's voice. Don't be afraid to reveal yourself.

Remember Who You Are: A Novelist's Story

I've known Meera for many years; we met decades ago when we were both beginning writers in San Jose. We hung out at writers conferences and participated in writers workshops and read our work aloud to each other in writers' groups. Meera was one of the most interesting people I knew; originally a farm girl from Missouri, she'd traveled the world in search of enlightenment. When I became an acquisitions editor for a mind/body/spirit imprint, I sought out Meera to write books for the new line—and she made a career for herself as the author of nonfiction titles, wonderful how-to books on the secrets of living an authentic life.

writing with quiet hands

She wrote fiction, too—fabulous stories starring the exotic people and places she'd met on her travels. While technically proficient, these stories fell flat on the page. Meera was imitating the voices of other cultures, other customs, other writers—and drowning out her own voice in the process. In the meantime, she moved to the country and settled on a little farm in Northern California she called the Henny Penny Farmette. She started blogging about her chickens, bees, and goats.

Her blog was a big hit—and the ammunition I needed to convince her to write a novel set on the Henny Penny Farmette. She'd found her fictive voice right there on the farm. (Of course, she'd never lost it; she used it when writing nonfiction. But her love of other cultures and faraway lands blinded her to it in her own storytelling.) She wrote the first in a traditional mystery series set on the farmette—and I got her a three-book deal. (Look for *Beeline to Murder: A Henny Penny Farmette Mystery* by Meera Lester, wherever you buy your books.)

VOICE LESSON #2: If you're having trouble finding your voice, start close to home. The truth is often right under your nose.

Listen to the Sound of Your Own Voice: The Historian's Story

When I first moved to Massachusetts, I had no writer friends, and even though I was working at a publishing house with book people, I missed hanging out with writers. (Editors are not the same as writers, though I love editors—especially editors who are *also* writers.) So I joined the online chapter of Mystery Writers of America and started interacting with the other members online.

There I bonded with fellow Rainer Maria Rilke–fan Brian Thornton, who was from the Northwest (and not the same Brian who writes police procedurals—my world is full of great writers named Brian). We became fast friends and met in person several times at writers conferences. Brian, a history teacher by day, even wrote a couple of great history-related nonfiction books for me while I was an acquisitions editor.

But what Brian really wanted to do was publish fiction. We exchanged some stories for critique. I read Brian's modern private-eye novel and one of his historical mystery stories. I told him that he should focus on historical fiction, as his historian's voice seemed better suited for it. Commercial historical fiction is not easy to write; only people who are passionate about it and can make it relevant to the modern reader succeed. The good news is that if you can write solid historical fiction, you can usually get published. So I wasn't at all surprised when Brian sold his first piece, a historical short story, to *Alfred Hitchcock's Mystery Magazine*. Now he's working on a historical mystery—and now I'm an agent—so here's hoping that he lets me shop it when he's ready. (Did I mention that I love being right?)

VOICE LESSON #3: Capitalize on your voice's strengths. Not only can this help refine your work, it can help you sell it.

Do Not Confuse Voice with Plot: The Artiste's Story

Sometimes I'm so bowled over by a writer's talent that I ignore the lack of market potential for the work and sign the writer anyway. That's what happened when I read Richard's writing for the first time. Richard's talent was obvious, and I wasn't the only one who thought so; he'd been celebrated for his brilliant short stories. But he'd yet to break into commercial fiction with his novels.

Richard's work was überdark—and überdark is not an easy sell. Even your *True Detective* stories have some (wan) light at the end of the dark tunnel of prose. I warned Richard about this, and he did some revision as requested, but he resisted my appeals to explore his not-so-darn-dark side. Eventually I caved—and I sent out the novel as it was to all the editors I knew who loved dark material. One by one they passed, saying it was just too dark, even for them. But if he wrote anything else, they'd love to see it.

I didn't give up. (I hate giving up.) I knew that we just needed to find an editor who'd fall in love with Richard's work the way I had. And I'm happy to say that we did; it took two years, but finally I got Richard a two-book deal with a Big Five house.

Unsurprisingly, the editor wanted a little (wan) light at the end of the dark tunnel of prose. Richard balked. The editor called me, and I called Richard. Richard was worried about "compromising his voice."

But voice really had nothing to do with it. If he found an audience, he couldn't risk engaging them with his compelling voice only to lose them at the end of the story by refusing to make a slight shift in plot from a "so dark you can't see" ending to a "dark but not so dark you have to slit your wrists" ending. I explained to him that the first page sells the book and the last page sells the next book. He didn't have to change his voice; he just had to rethink the emotional impact of the ending on his reader. Leaving a bad taste in the reader's mouth—no matter how beautiful the voice—is not the way to build an audience. (Richard Thomas's novel *Disintegration* recently debuted to great reviews and endorsements by such literary lights as Chuck Palahniuk, Irvine Welsh, Chuck Wendig, Paul Tremblay, and more.)

VOICE LESSON #4: Voice is how you tell the story—it's not the story itself. Be sure that you don't compromise the emotional impact of your story to protect what you mistakenly believe is your voice.

***

Ultimately, the challenge is this: Figure out who you are and what you care about, and let your voice reveal both.

In the next chapter, we'll explore how the subtleties of style and substance can enhance your voice and your storytelling.

HANDS ON

Create a mantra customized to enhance your voice. This mantra should address whatever issues are keeping you from expressing yourself freely:

- *I allow the truth to speak through me.*
- *I sing my own song.*
- *I listen to my true self, and I hear the truth of others.*
- *I say what I need to say when I need to say it.*
- *I am free to tell my truth, as others are free to tell their truths.*

Post this in your writing space to remind you that your voice deserves to be heard.

CHAPTER FIVE

style and substance

"He who has nothing to assert has no style and can have none." —GEORGE BERNARD SHAW

Two elements that characterize the accomplished writer's work are style and substance. No matter what the genre, style and substance are the hallmarks of the professional writer. Other aspects of quality storytelling being equal, they can make the difference between a good writer and a great writer.

In this chapter we'll look at the parts that make up the whole of style and substance, from tone to mission. Let's start with substance— because if the words you write don't say anything, the words you write don't matter.

NOW THAT'S SAYING SOMETHING

"All we have is the story we tell. Everything we do, every decision we make, our strength, weakness, motivation, history, and character—what we believe—none of it is real; it's all part of the story we tell. But here's the thing: It's our goddamned story!" —JESS WALTER

Write what you know. We've all heard this conventional wisdom before, starting with Mark Twain and nearly every writing instructor we've encountered since. Writing what you know is solid advice, if somewhat limiting. To paraphrase Howard Nemerov, if you only write what you know, that may leave you with a lot of free time.

Expanding that advice, sound as it may be, gives you more room in which to create. So try this broader version on for size:

Write what you know.

Write what you love.

Write what you'd love to know.

A QUESTION OF CRAFT

What do you know? What do you love? What would you love to know?

Remember the exercise we did in the previous chapter, in which you created a bubble chart designed to help you find your true voice? You identified many aspects about yourself that you could use to uncover it. Now let's dive deeper to reveal how you might use what you know, what you love, and what you'd love to know to give your work substance.

Using the bubble chart on the next page, jot down at least two entries for the lists on a separate sheet of paper. Do this quickly; don't think about it. When you're finished, consider what you've discovered in this process.

The Art of Fielding: **A Short Case Study**

Chad Harbach's novel *The Art of Fielding* is about college baseball shortstop genius Henry Skrimshander, who seems destined for the big leagues until a routine throw goes rogue—and changes the lives of five people forever.

When I first read this wonderful baseball novel—I admit to being a sucker for any baseball novel that's about more than baseball—I was reminded that the best stories reflect their authors' knowledge, background, and obsessions. I suspected that Chad Harbach had traded heavily on this useful triumvirate in the writing of his novel.

Let's take a look at what Harbach's substance bubble chart might look like, based on what's in *The Art of Fielding.*

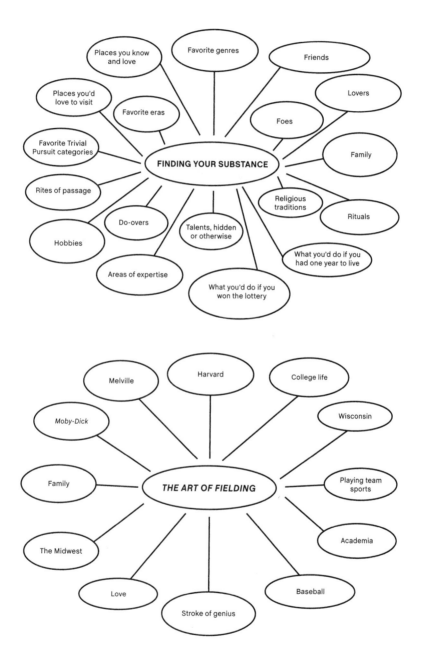

FINDING YOUR SUBSTANCE

- Places you know and love
- Favorite genres
- Friends
- Places you'd love to visit
- Favorite eras
- Lovers
- Foes
- Favorite Trivial Pursuit categories
- Family
- Rites of passage
- Religious traditions
- Rituals
- Do-overs
- Hobbies
- Talents, hidden or otherwise
- What you'd do if you had one year to live
- Areas of expertise
- What you'd do if you won the lottery

THE ART OF FIELDING

- Melville
- Harvard
- College life
- Moby-Dick
- Wisconsin
- Family
- Playing team sports
- The Midwest
- Academia
- Love
- Baseball
- Stroke of genius

After reading *The Art of Fielding,* I would have bet money that Harbach was from the Midwest, played baseball as a kid, went to Harvard, and loved *Moby-Dick.* And I would have won: Harbach grew up in Wisconsin, went to Harvard, earned an MFA at the University of Virginia, helped found the literary journal *n + 1,* and still loves the Brewers and *Moby-Dick.*

This is how you spin the threads of your own knowledge, background, and history into gold, as Harbach has done. Read *The Art of Fielding*—and ask yourself how you can do the same thing in your work. (And keep in mind that Harbach received an estimated $650,000 advance for his novel.)

"What fascinates me about baseball is that although it's a team game, and a team becomes a kind of family, the players on the field are each very much alone. Your teammates depend on you and support you, but at the moments that count they can't bail you out." —CHAD HARBACH

TONING IT UP—AND DOWN

Style and tone are two of the storyteller's more subtle tools; the right tone and style can help bring a story to life. Yet writers often confuse the two; it's easy to mistake one for the other, or either or both for voice. Let's define our terms.

With your *voice,* you express your truth as a storyteller.

With your *tone,* you communicate the emotion, atmosphere, and mood of your story.

With your *style,* you articulate your story and give form to that expression.

Think of it this way: Your voice is your personality, the character traits and personal qualities and unalienable truths that make up who you are, day in and day out, through good times and bad. Your tone is your mood, your emotional state, which can change from light to dark, sweet to bitter, happy to sad, depending on what's happening in your life. Your style is how you move through the world, the way you wear your hat and choose your clothes and strut your stuff.

Let's take a look at voice, tone, and style as displayed in the opening of Edgar Allan Poe's "The Fall of the House of Usher."

> During the whole of a dull, dark, and soundless day in the autumn of the year, when the clouds hung oppressively low in the heavens, I had been passing alone, on horseback, to a singularly dreary tract of country; and at length found myself, as the shades of the evening drew on, within view of the melancholy House of Usher.

- **VOICE:** Edgar Allan Poe is known for his horror and mystery stories, like this one. He tells his tales of death and decay, murder and mourning, in a macabre, almost hypnotic voice.
- **TONE:** The mood Poe creates here is one of suspense and dread. Poe unsettles his readers by means of atmosphere; we know bad things are going to happen. The narrator is riding straight into darkness.
- **STYLE:** This long first line exemplifies Poe's use of tightly constructed, complex sentences, alliteration, and internal rhyme, a style that suits the disturbing stories he is known for—and "The Fall of the House of Usher" is no exception.

Consider the opening line(s) from one of your stories. How would you describe the voice, the tone, and the style? How do these elements enhance one another—or not?

Now that you understand exactly what voice, tone, and style are and how they interrelate, let's take a harder look at tone and style, as we have already done for voice.

Tone

"I think striking the right tone for your story is, if you like, the alchemical work of writing."

—JULIA LEIGH

As we've seen, tone speaks to the emotion, atmosphere, and mood of your work. Regardless of genre, writers known for their tone endear themselves to agents, editors, and readers. Finding the right tone for your story is hitting the right note, as these writers do from their opening lines:

> When I was a little girl I used to dress Barbie up without underpants. On the outside, she'd look like the perfect lady. Tasteful plastic heels, tailored suit. But underneath, she was naked.
>
> —*High Five* by Janet Evanovich

Evanovich begins the fifth entry in her popular Stephanie Plum series with the trademark smart-ass Jersey-girl tone, which charms the reader into accompanying the brash and brassy bounty hunter from Trenton on another madcap adventure. The tone is fast and funny and in your face, just like her heroine.

> He has forgotten something, he knows that for sure when he wakes up. Something he dreamt during the night. Something he ought to remember.
>
> —*Faceless Killers* by Henning Mankell

The tone is as spare and bleak as the Scandinavian landscape in the first lines of Swedish writer Henning Mankell's best-selling Wallander series. It prepares the reader for the chronic pessimism that plagues his hero, Wallander, in particular and his country in general.

> I was in a coffee shop looking through the want ads when I read, "Macy's Herald Square, the largest store in the world, has big opportunities for outgoing, fun-loving people of all shapes and sizes who want more than just a holiday job! Working as an elf in Macy's SantaLand means being at the center of the excitement ... ."
> I circled the ad and then I laughed out loud at the thought of it.
> —*Holidays on Ice* by David Sedaris

David Sedaris has made his mark as a storyteller of wit and woe, whose tales are told in a tone as poignant as it is funny. We know from these opening lines that our hapless hero will put on that suit—and terrible, funny, and terribly funny antics will ensue.

> No live organism can continue for long to exist sanely under conditions of absolute reality; even larks and katydids are supposed, by some, to dream. Hill House, not sane, stood by itself against its hills, holding darkness within; it had stood so for eighty years and might stand for eighty more.
> —*The Haunting of Hill House* by Shirley Jackson

It's all there in these first few lines: a crazy house willing to kill anything, perhaps even larks and katydids. I don't mind saying that this novel scared the crap out of me. I was thinking about writing a ghost story at the time—more *Blythe Spirit* than *The Haunting of Hill House*. I don't know why I thought I should read it for research, since I knew from the tone Jackson set in the very beginning that I was in Edgar Allan Poe territory and would undoubtedly suffer many sleepless nights after reading it. Which I did.

> A thunderclap preceded sudden hard-driving rain, blotting out the shots, two insignificant little bangs compared to the divine anger bursting forth, booming in splendor. When the rain fell, IJsbreker fell too. The rain splashed on the windowsill, into the open window

on the body and the floor. Outside it lashed at the tarmac, houseboats, and parked cars, whipped trembling leaves on gigantic elms, cut into the quiet water of the canal, split myriad tiny waves that the sudden storm brushed up.

—*Hard Rain* by Janwillem Van De Wetering

Dutch writer Van De Wetering came of age during World War II and was so disturbed by the horrific events of that conflict that he went in search of answers while traveling the world on business for his father's company. He ended up in a Zen monastery in Kyoto, Japan. He came home a Buddhist, worked for the Dutch police force as a special constabulary, and wrote a series of acclaimed detective novels. Van De Wetering's tone reflects his Zen studies, recalling the lyrical simplicity of a koan and carrying the pitch-perfect lessons of nonattachment.

In all of these examples, the writer has worked to achieve a tone that distinguishes the story right away and puts the reader in a suitable mood for the journey ahead. Sit down and get comfortable, the tone says to the reader, and settle in for a good, funny, scary, poignant, disturbing, or enlightening—but always unforgettable—ride.

That's why the right tone is critical to your work. How do you want your readers to feel as they read your story? What are the emotional highs and lows you want them to experience? How can your tone help evoke those feelings?

Other writers whose tone is pitch-perfect include:

- Voltaire
- Anne Rice
- Jonathan Swift
- William Faulkner
- Anaïs Nin
- Helen Fielding
- Emily Brontë
- Henry James
- Edith Wharton
- John Steinbeck
- Jane Austen

Say you're writing a love story. If you're writing a sad story, your tone could be sentimental, as in *Love Story* by Erich Segal, a tearjerker whose beloved heroine Jennifer brought that name back into fashion with a vengeance. If you're writing a happier story, where the girl gets the guy (eventually), then your tone could be hilarious and self-deprecating, like the tone of Helen Fielding's *Bridget Jones's Diary*. Or maybe you're writing a twisted love story, where the couple truly deserves each other and will go to deadly lengths to prove it—as in *Gone Girl* by Gillian Flynn, written in a tone that's as dark and devious as the story itself.

Study the tone in stories by authors in your genre—and deconstruct how they build that tone to evoke the atmosphere, emotion, and mood. Think about how you can achieve the same effects.

HANDS ON

Choose a best-selling book in your genre whose tone is similar to the one you are trying to achieve in your story. Copy the first page of that novel in longhand. Now write (or rewrite) the first page of your story in the same tone. Compare the two. Do they sound similar? Do they both create the same atmosphere? Set the same mood? Evoke the same feeling?

"When you read Chekhov, everything has an even gray tone. When you read [my novel] *Family Life*, everything has an even white tone. It is almost like when you paint on paper and you can see the paper through the paint." —AKHIL SHARMA

Style

"There is such an animal as a nonstylist, only they're not writers—they're typists." —TRUMAN CAPOTE

As we've seen, style speaks to the form of your expression; it's the actual way in which you put words together, structure your sentences, and use punctuation. It's the words you choose—and why you choose to use them. The right style enhances your story, just as wearing the right clothes on the outside can reflect who you are on the inside.

Let's take a look at some of the writers who are known for a style so unique it's identifiable from word one.

> I sent one boy to the gas chamber at Huntsville. One and only one. My arrest and my testimony. I went up there and visited with him two or three times. Three times. The last time was the day of his execution. I didnt have to go but I did. I sure didnt want to.
> —*No Country for Old Men* by Cormac McCarthy

Pulitzer Prize–winning author Cormac McCarthy tells his dark and violent stories—*No Country for Old Men, The Road,* and the Border trilogy—in what *The Boston Globe* called "stripped down, doom-soaked prose." As you can see in the opening lines of *No Country for Old Men,* his nihilistic, poetic style is rife with alliteration and repetition and a kind of rhythm that scares readers even as it pulls them into the story. McCarthy writes by his own set of punctuation rules, which by his own admission consist mostly of periods, capitals, and the odd comma. He leaves out a lot of conventional punctuation, notably quotation marks and the apostrophes in contractions.

> Here is an account of a few years in the life of Quoyle, born in Brooklyn and raised in a shuffle of dreary upstate towns.
> Hive-spangled, gut roaring with gas and cramp, he survived childhood; at the state university, hand clapped over his chin, he camouflaged torment with smiles and silence. Stumbled through his twenties and into his thirties learning to separate his feelings from his life, counting on nothing. He ate prodigiously, liked a ham knuckle, buttered spuds.
> —*The Shipping News* by Annie Proulx

The New York Times called reading Proulx like "bouncing along rutted country roads in a pickup truck with no shock absorbers." But there's a muscular lyricism that lulls the reader like a great country-western song. Proulx has a penchant for odd names and weird nouns, which she weaves in and out of her sentences in an alliterative rhythm that, in its own way, is as hypnotic as Poe's prose.

> Once upon a time and a very good time it was there was a moocow coming down along the road and this moocow that was coming down along the road met a nicens little boy named baby tuckoo …
> His father told him that story: his father looked at him through a glass: he had a hairy face.
> —*A Portrait of the Artist as a Young Man* by James Joyce

James Joyce is one of those writers whose style is so singular that it takes the world by storm—in its own time and for generations to come. His experimental, stream-of-consciousness style is as playful and unpredictable as it is poetic and poignant. Joyce's boldness with language has, as Goethe would say, "genius, magic, and power in it"; his lyrical, fantastical prose washes over you like a dream. This no-holds-barred approach to style is one that all writers could learn from, if only to give ourselves permission to let go and let the words flow—and see what bubbles up.

Every genre contains great writers known for their style:

- Ernest Hemingway
- Virginia Woolf
- William Faulkner
- David Foster Wallace
- Salmon Rushdie
- Isabel Allende
- Mark Leyner
- Charles Bukowski
- Douglas Adams
- Annie Dillard
- Tom Robbins
- Pat Conroy
- Kurt Vonnegut
- Alice Hoffman
- Joyce Carol Oates

- Raymond Chandler
- Gertrude Stein
- David Mamet

We all can't be Cormac McCarthy or Annie Proulx or James Joyce—and we shouldn't try. Your writing style should suit your chosen subject matter. This marriage of style and substance leads to the most successful storytelling.

If you're writing a gothic story set primarily in nineteenth-century New Orleans about love and alienation and vampires, your style could be lyrical and lush and lurid, as Anne Rice's style in the best-selling *Interview with the Vampire* has been called.

If you're writing a novel set in Arkansas in the 1870s about a fourteen-year-old girl out for vengeance, your style could be as resolute and unsentimental as its heroine, recalling the era in which it takes place through long, rolling sentences and narrative formality—just as Charles Portis does in his classic *True Grit*.

If you're writing a novel about the excesses of the eighties, your style might be as over the top and bombastic as the decade itself, making full use of colorful and satirical language that pulls out all the stops, dropping brand names and exclamation points freely, as Tom Wolfe does in his bestseller *The Bonfire of the Vanities* (originally serialized in *Rolling Stone* magazine in twenty-seven installments).

Or maybe you're writing a private-eye novel about a wisecracking detective in 1940s Los Angeles, so your style combines the force of a blunt instrument with the wit of clever, biting similes, as Raymond Chandler does in his hard-boiled classic *Farewell, My Lovely*.

Study the style in stories by authors in your genre—and analyze how they use the language, choose their words, construct their sentences, and set their rhythms. Think about how you can achieve the same effects.

ON STYLE

Here are some of the best books on style, from writers who know what they are talking about:

- *The Elements of Style* by William Strunk Jr., E.B. White, and Roger Angell
- *The Writing Life* by Annie Dillard
- "How to Write with Style" by Kurt Vonnegut
- *On Writing Well* by William Zinsser
- *Writing Tools* by Roy Peter Clark
- *Writing with Style* by John R. Trimble
- *Three Uses of the Knife: On the Nature and Purpose of Drama* by David Mamet
- *Ernest Hemingway on Writing* edited by Larry W. Phillips
- *How to Write a Sentence* by Stanley Fish
- *How to Write* by Gertrude Stein

HANDS ON

This is the style version of the exercise you did previously for tone. Choose a best-selling book in your genre whose style is similar to the one you are trying to achieve in your story. Copy the first page of that novel in longhand. Now write (or rewrite) the first page of your story in the same style. Compare the two—in terms of sentence structure, word choice, alliteration, internal rhyme, rhythm, and punctuation. What comes naturally to you? What can you adopt going forward?

CLARITY: THE ULTIMATE IN STYLE

"I made up my mind long ago to follow one cardinal rule in all my writing—to be clear. I have given up all thought of writing poetically or symbolically or experimentally, or in any of the other modes that might (if I were good enough) get me a Pulitzer Prize. I would write merely clearly and in this way establish a warm relationship between myself and my readers, and the professional critics—Well, they can do whatever they wish." —ISAAC ASIMOV

For many writers, clarity is the first—and sometimes only—aim. Your tone and style should strike clear notes. The goal: clear and concise prose.

I have a client named Greg who's a stand-up comedian. He writes his own stuff and is one of the funniest people I have ever met. He's quick, and that quickness serves him well on stage, where he can turn a heckler's taunts into the most hilarious bit in his already hilarious act. The audience loves him.

But when he wanted to write a book, those improvisation skills didn't necessarily translate. Being funny on the page is not the same as being funny on the stage. You need a funny premise and funny characters, to be sure, just as you do on the stage, but for the page you also need to achieve (1) a tone that's humorous, ironic, or satirical and (2) a style that incorporates wordplay and rhythm to comic advantage. Most important, you need to be perfectly clear, because if your readers have to stop to think about what you mean, you've lost them. Obscurity is not funny; hitting your mark is.

My client mastered comedic tone and style, learned the art of being funny on the page, and wrote a best-selling humor series. (Look for the WTF? series by Gregory Bergman wherever you buy your books.) Now he's making movies, where he can use all the tools of humor—literary, visual, aural, dramatic, and so on—at his disposal. Wordplay *and* sight gags, if you will. What he learned about clarity through writing humor books applies regardless of medium.

Letting Go

As we've seen in this chapter, the best work has style *and* substance. You want your stories to be *about* something meaningful, and you can use voice, tone, and style to bring that meaning to life.

Now it's time to let go—and dramatize it.

PART TWO

pen meets paper

pen

noun \\'pen\\

: an implement for writing or drawing with ink or a similar fluid

"writing implement," late 13c., from Old French *pene* "quill pen; feather" (12c.) and directly from Latin *penna* "a feather, plume," in plural "a wing," in Late Latin, "a pen for writing," from Old Latin *petna*, *pesna*, from *pet-na-*, suffixed form of root *pet-* "to rush; to fly"

pa·per

noun \\'pā-pər\\

: the material that is used in the form of thin sheets for writing or printing on, wrapping things, etc.

Mid-14c., from Anglo-French *paper*, Old French *papier* "paper, document," from Latin *papyrus* "paper, paper made of papyrus stalks"

CHAPTER SIX

the construction of story

"Wherever a story comes from, whether it is a familiar myth or a private memory, the retelling exemplifies the making of a connection from one pattern to another: a potential translation in which narrative becomes parable and the once upon a time comes to stand for some renascent truth."
—MARY CATHERINE BATESON

Ideas for stories are everywhere: a scrap of overheard conversation here, an unexpected encounter there. Maybe it's a dream or a memory or a vision that speaks to you. Or maybe you are driven by a need for justice or revenge or your own happy ending.

You may start with a character, a question, or a place. Best-selling author Dean Koontz, who's sold some 450 million copies of his many novels worldwide, says that the idea for his popular Odd Thomas series occurred to him while he was writing another book: "Into my head came the line, 'My name is Odd Thomas. I lead an unusual life.'" Koontz listened and followed the short-order cook who sees dead people through six novels and a few prequels as well. Twenty million copies later, Odd Thomas remains one of Koontz's most-beloved characters.

For John Green, the best-selling author of such young adult classics as *The Fault in Our Stars* and *An Abundance of Katherines*, a philosophical question sometimes leads him into a story. In *Looking for Alaska*, Green was exploring the nature of suffering, which began, he says, in "thinking about whether there was meaning to suffering and how one can reconcile one's self to a world where suffering is so unjustly distributed." I won't even try to expand on that statement; you'll have to read the book to see how he pulls it off. There's a reason this novel—his first—established Green as a unique voice, inviting comparisons to J.D. Salinger.

Alice Hoffman, whose novels are usually inspired by fairy tales, had no plans to write a historical novel when she went to Israel and visited Masada, the ancient fortress that sits high on a plateau at the far eastern end of the desert in Judea, overlooking the Dead Sea. But she knew as soon as she stepped inside she must write a story set in Masada during the Roman siege of the fortification in 73 c.e., in which hundreds of Jewish rebels hiding out there committed suicide rather than surrender. "At Masada," said Hoffman, "I felt the nearness of the past and felt as though I could hear the voices of the women who had lived there so long ago." The result: *The Dovekeepers,* Hoffman's deeply researched story of four women struggling for survival during the siege, her most ambitious and acclaimed work to date.

A QUESTION OF CRAFT

Figuring out which ideas can sustain a story—not to mention your own interest—is the exciting part. Think of it as speed dating for writers: Which ideas do you really like? Which are too fussy or fickle or frenetic for you? Which would you follow into hell—and back?

DREAMING THE ARCHITECTURE

"Writing a story or a novel is one way of discovering sequence in experience, of stumbling upon cause

and effect in the happenings of a writer's own life."
—EUDORA WELTY

So you've gotten an idea for a story. An image or a voice haunts you, or a place or a person whose story you need to tell. Now you just have to figure out how to tell it.

You start by capturing on paper whatever impulse is driving you to the page. Then, like a child building a sandcastle on the beach, you play with it. You use your tools—sand, water, spade, pail, rake, seashells—to construct a chateau room by room, adding towers and moats and ramparts as you go. You know what a castle looks like, and odds are, this isn't your first beach rodeo.

But when you court an idea with the intention of transforming it into a story, you may not be so sure what a story looks like—and it may very well be your first story rodeo. And even if this isn't your first story, it's the first time you're telling *this* particular tale. Most writers take on more challenging material with each book—and you are probably no exception. Don't be surprised if what worked for the last novel doesn't work for the next one.

As an agent, I see project after project fail to sell because the structure of the story doesn't work.

The right framework for your story—that is, the structure that will best support your idea—is critical to its success. And without it, your chances of selling your work are slim, no matter how accomplished the writing or how unique the idea. Even projects that do sell must undergo editing during the publishing process, and that editing is often related to structure. (I could write an entire book on the topic of structure alone—and I did. *Plot Perfect* is available wherever you buy your books.)

Getting structure right is as simple—and as difficult—as finding the right way to tell your story. Here are some tools to play around with the structure of your story.

What If?

"I love the dreaming phase, thinking up the story and playing around with ideas and characters. I

love the 'what ifs ...' What if this happened? What if that happened? One idea sparks off another, and very soon the basis of a story is flying around in my head."
—GILL LEWIS

The "what if?" exercise can prove one of the most painless and productive means of brainstorming ways of structuring your story. The trick is to let your imagination run wild. The wilder your "what ifs?" the better. Let your inner creator drive the process—and kick your inner editor to the curb.

What if:

- fossilized DNA could be used to re-create dinosaurs? (*Jurassic Park* by Michael Crichton)
- an English nurse was transported back in time to Scotland? (*Outlander* by Diana Gabaldon)
- a doctor could talk to animals? (*Doctor Dolittle* by Hugh Lofting)
- a boy and a girl from feuding families fell in love? (*Romeo and Juliet* by William Shakespeare)
- a Soviet submarine commander decided to defect? (*The Hunt for Red October* by Tom Clancy)
- an old fisherman took on a giant marlin? (*The Old Man and the Sea* by Ernest Hemingway)

You might try playing the "what if?" game with a friend or a fellow writer. When it comes to brainstorming, two heads are often better than one. Just be sure that you choose someone you trust completely, someone who is supportive of your work, understands the nature of brainstorming (there are no stupid ideas), and can be relied on to be discreet (you can't copyright ideas, and you don't want yours blabbed all over the blogosphere).

Voice and Place

"But once the voice comes, the 'here' comes next, and then the 'something happened'—what we call plot—follows from it. ... If you are lucky enough to find voice and place, there are real consequences to those choices. Together, they limit the possibilities of what can possibly come next—and they help point the way forward." —Linn Ullmann

If a character is speaking to you, just as the voices spoke to Alice Hoffman at Masada, you've found the voice of your novel. And just as those voices could only have come from Masada, the voice you hear comes from somewhere, too. You know who and where. Now all you need to do is figure out what happens when you put that character in that place.

What happens when ...

- Dorothy isn't in Kansas anymore? (*The Wonderful Wizard of Oz* by L. Frank Baum)
- defense attorney Perry Mason practices law in Los Angeles? (*The Case of the Velvet Claws* by Erle Stanley Gardner)
- Jane Eyre accepts a position at Thornfield? (*Jane Eyre* by Charlotte Brontë)
- a group of British schoolboys crash on an island? (*Lord of the Flies* by William Golding)
- Emma Bovary marries a country doctor? (*Madame Bovary* by Gustave Flaubert)
- Sheriff Longmire enforces the law in Wyoming? (*The Cold Dish* by Craig Johnson)

What happens to your characters when you put them in their place? What happens next? And then what happens?

I have a client from New England who's been vacationing on St. John for years. After writing a couple of crime novels that went nowhere, she gave her Bostonian heroine a troubled past, ran her out of town, and plopped her on St. John, where she runs an inn and stumbles across dead bodies. Voice and character plus place equals plot—and now my client has a multi-book deal for her traditional mystery series. (Look for *No Virgin Island* by C. Michele Dorsey wherever you buy your books.)

Beg, Borrow, Steal

"I think that that idea of reinvention [for *Blue Diary*] originally sprang from the fairy tale of Bluebeard and the idea of someone reinventing themselves or turning out to be not what you think they are. I was reading different versions of that fairy tale and talking about it with other women, feeling that it was a really resonant fairy tale for a lot of people. The original fairy tale was about the youngest sister going into a room in the castle and finding all the bodies of the wives that came before her—she is confronted with truth, thinking about how often we think we know people and we really don't."
—ALICE HOFFMAN

If you're having trouble coming up with a plot, consider pinching one. You can beg, borrow, or outright steal from a storyline from a classic that's stood the test of time—and is now in the public domain. Myths and legends, Shakespearean plays, fairy tales, nursery rhymes, and nineteenth-century novels are all potential sources for cool stories. As an agent who pitches novels for a living, I can tell you that two of every acquisitions editor's favorite words are "modern retelling."

Consider a modern retelling of:

- Greek mythology (*The Lightning Thief* by Rick Riordan).
- *Romeo and Juliet* (*Julie and Romeo* by Jeanne Ray).
- *The Picture of Dorian Gray* (*Dorian, an Imitation* by Will Self).
- *King Lear* (*A Thousand Acres* by Jane Smiley).
- *Wuthering Heights* (*Here on Earth* by Alice Hoffman).
- the Tristan and Isolde legend (*Brazil* by John Updike).

Some authors, not content to merely retell these stories, reinvent them. Gregory Maguire, author of the bestseller *Wicked*, rewrote

The Wonderful Wizard of Oz from the Wicked Witch's point of view. David Wroblewski penned *The Story of Edgar Sawtelle*, best described as *Hamlet*—with dogs. Seth Grahame-Smith added zombies to Jane Austen's classic *Pride and Prejudice* in *Pride and Prejudice and Zombies*, creating a whole new mash-up subgenre in the process.

Apparently, *Pride and Prejudice* is a gold mine for today's novelists. Goodreads features a list of 238 books inspired by *Pride and Prejudice*, from Helen Fielding's *Bridget Jones's Diary* to Linda Berdoll's *Mr. Darcy Takes a Wife*. If you think you can write no. 239, more power to you!

WRITE IT DOWN

Get a pen and some paper, and set a timer for fifteen minutes. Take out the substance bubble chart you made in chapter five and brainstorm ways in which you could use those elements in your storyline. Use the "what ifs?" and "voice and place" tools.

FRAMING THE BUILDING

To paraphrase Winston Churchill, we shape our stories, and afterwards our stories shape us. Finding the right structure for your story can not only help you tell the story, it will affect how you tell it, and the very story you tell.

Some of you are plotters by nature. Your story ideas are plot ideas rather than ideas borne of character or voice or place. You may have other obstacles to overcome—creating well-rounded characters, weaving in theme, etc.—which we'll address later on, but structure isn't one of them. Lucky you.

But those of you who work from character, voice, and/or place may find plotting a challenge. You may find yourself writing slice-of-life stories, in which very little actually happens. This is fine if you'll be satisfied publishing your work in literary journals or self-publishing. (And there's nothing wrong with either of those options.) But if you want to publish commercial fiction with a traditional publisher, you'll need a compelling storyline with a beginning, a middle, and an end.

Together these three parts—beginning, middle, end—make up the classic three-act structure. We tell stories with this structure intuitively; we begin with "once upon a time" and end with "and they lived happily ever after." Don't overthink this formula; it's as easy as "boy meets girl, boy loses girl, boy gets girl back."

Before you get too caught up in the three-act structure of your story, think about the time frame in which the story occurs: Where and when will you choose to enter the story, and where and when will you choose to leave it? What events will you dramatize in between the entrance and the exit?

Setting the time parameters of your story can help you devise a strong storyline. Aristotle believed that the most compelling stories took place within a single twenty-four-hour period, and, generally speaking, the shorter the time frame, the better. But you can make any time frame work, as the authors of the following stories have done successfully:

- *The Hours* by Michael Cunningham
- *One Day in the Life of Ivan Denisovich* by Aleksandr Solzhenitsyn
- *A Christmas Carol* by Charles Dickens
- *The Longest Day* by Cornelius Ryan
- *The Lost Weekend* by Charles Jackson
- *Gaudy Night* by Dorothy L. Sayers
- *The Enchanted April* by Elizabeth von Arnim
- *The Forty Days of Musa Dagh* by Franz Werfel
- *Summer of My German Soldier* by Bette Greene
- *My Losing Season* by Pat Conroy
- *The Long Winter* by Laura Ingalls Wilder
- *A Year in Provence* by Peter Mayle
- *The Brief Wondrous Life of Oscar Wao* by Junot Díaz

Choosing a time frame for your story—again, the shorter, the better—can help you focus your work on the most critical events of the story. Every book is a journey—and if you prolong the journey with asides and flashbacks and detours, you risk alienating your readers, who want you to get on with the story. Readers know when you're off track, when you're dawdling by the side of the road, and when you've lost your way. Deciding on a tight time frame—and sticking to it—streamlines your story and keeps your reader turning the pages.

One of my clients, Kate Defrise, wrote a charming novel about a Belgian-American family of grown siblings who've moved away and grown apart after their mother died. Their father went through several wives afterward. Her original draft takes place over the course of a year and culminates in a tense Christmas dinner at the patriarch's house, at which emotions run high, secrets are revealed, and the fate of the familial bond hangs in the balance. An editor expressed interest but was reluctant to commit to buying the project because of structural issues. She asked if the author would rework the structure, shrinking the time frame to just a couple of months before Christmas. The author, as advised by *moi*, agreed.

Cutting the time frame focused the story, sharpened the pacing, and intensified the emotional impact on the reader. The restructured story was also now more commercial. Whenever you build a story around a major holiday—Christmas, Valentine's Day, the Fourth of July, even Father's Day—you gain promotional opportunities at booksellers and elsewhere that would otherwise be unavailable to you, opportunities that can help establish your name. I resubmitted the story to that same editor—and got a two-book deal for my client. (Look for *Christmas Chocolat* by Kate Defrise wherever you buy your books.)

DRILL IT DOWN

Think about your story's time frame. How would you tell your story over the course of a year? A day? A week? A month? A decade? A lifetime?

GILDING THE GENRE

"What monster sleeps in the deep of your story? You need a monster. Without a monster there is no story."
—BILLY MARSHALL

The best advice I can give you on story structure: Know your genre. I'll repeat that, not just because I always repeat my best advice but because I am always astounded by the number of writers who do not know their genre. Or if they do know it, they do not use that knowledge when they plot their own stories.

Know your own genre.

No worries, you say. That's not *me:* I write mysteries, and I know my genre. I've been reading Agatha Christie since I was twelve years old.

Swell—but how many of today's *new,* best-selling mystery writers have you read? I'm talking about writers who are (1) still alive and (2) have published either their *debut* novels or their *breakout* novels within the past five years to great success. These are the stories you should pay attention to—not just reading them, but *studying* them.

I've been an agent for a couple of years now. When I first started shopping crime fiction, all I heard from editors was: *I'm looking for the next Tana French.* A year later: *I'm looking for the next* Gone Girl. *Or the next* Defending Jacob. *Something with "an edge."*

The same holds true for other genres as well: *I'm looking for the next Celeste Ng (literary fiction) or Erika Johansen (fantasy) or Emily St. John Mandel (science fiction) or Paula Hawkins (thriller).*

The debut writers in your genre are the writers you are competing against. The Sue Graftons and Stephen Kings and J.K. Rowlings of the world broke out and found their audiences years ago in a marketplace far different than the one all wannabe best-selling authors face today. They're not your competition; they're way beyond that.

You are seeking to break out in today's landscape, so you need to understand who is breaking out now—and how they are doing it. This is your competition. These are the writers whose stories you need to study. Figure out what made the difference in their stories. Which plot conventions of their genres did they follow? Which did they ignore, twist, tweak, or stand on their respective heads?

PLOT CONVENTIONS 101

Each genre has its own conventions:

- **ROMANCE** has its sexy but dangerous heroes, heartbroken but hopeful heroines, secret pasts, interfering mothers, supportive best friends, first kisses and first fights, misunderstandings and mistaken identities, and old boyfriends and jealous exes.
- **MYSTERY** has its multiple murders, usual suspects, false leads, red herrings, linguistic clues, and even "the butler did it" resolutions.

writing with quiet hands

- **SCIENCE FICTION** has its aliens and unexplored planets, an Earth dying or dead or under attack, humans and robots and clones and mutants, time travel and interstellar warfare.
- **FANTASY** has its kings and dragons and magic, witches and wizards, elves and dwarves and all manner of warriors, human and otherwise, fighting dark lords in medieval landscapes.

Make a serious study of the conventions in your genre. These are the conventions you need to play with when you structure your story. Follow them too closely and your work will not sell because it's too derivative. Ignore them completely and you'll antagonize your readers, who'll think you should know better. (And you should.)

Because what you don't know *can* hurt your story.

Take three of the best-selling debut or breakout novels published in your genre in the past three years. Outline their storylines scene by scene. Now compare and contrast. What have you learned that you can apply to your own storyline? Which conventions can you follow? Which can you ignore, twist, tweak, or stand on their respective heads?

Note: I know you don't want to do this. Nobody ever does. But if you do, you'll understand structure in a much deeper and more comprehensive way. If you want to cheat, then watch three films based on bestsellers in your genre. Make scene lists as you watch. Be sure to select movies that closely follow the plotlines of the novels on which they are based.

PLOT POINTS AND THE THREE-ACT STRUCTURE

You've probably heard of *plot points*, which is just a fancy term for the biggest scenes in your story. For example, if you are writing a love story, your plot points would look like this:

BEGINNING/ACT ONE/BOY MEETS GIRL
INCITING INCIDENT: Meet-cute
PLOT POINT 1: First kiss

MIDDLE/ACT TWO/BOY LOSES GIRL
MIDPOINT: First fight
PLOT POINT 2: Break up

END/ACT THREE/BOY GETS GIRL BACK
CLIMAX: Reconciliation
DENOUEMENT: Wedding

You've been mulling over the big story questions and the beginning, middle, and end of your story. Breaking down the three-act structure into these big scenes can help you ensure that you are building a compelling plot.

Do your homework, and you'll be prepared to structure your story. And when you do, you'll know enough to make yours different enough to stand apart—and find an audience.

"I like having a plot; I like characters with a reason to get up in the morning." —PETER TEMPLE

HANDS ON

Now you can map out your storyline. I like to do this with index cards. For a typical novel, you'll need at least sixty scenes: fifteen scenes for Act One, thirty scenes for Act Two, and fifteen scenes for Act Three. (If you've made scene lists for your comparable titles, you'll know about how many you'll need.) Now jot down ideas for scenes, scene by scene, making your way through the story. If you get stuck, start with the obligatory big scenes. For example, in a love story, these may include the meet-cute, the first date, the first sex, the first fight, the breakup, the reconciliation, and the wedding. For a mystery, obligatory scenes may include the first murder, the second murder, the crime scene, investigating suspects, confronting the murderer, and so on.

CHAPTER SEVEN

the resurrection
of character

"As a writer, I demand the right to write any character in the world that I want to write. I demand the
right to be them, I demand the right to think them,
and I demand the right to tell the truth as I see they
are." —QUENTIN TARANTINO

The most common complaint I hear from editors who pass on the stories I send them is this: *I just didn't connect with the character.* It isn't
easy to create heroes and heroines readers will follow for three hundred pages and then wait for expectantly in a subsequent novel. But it
is critical to your success as a storyteller.

And you can't stop at bringing your protagonist to life on the page;
the most endearing stories pitch their protagonists against worthy
antagonists who challenge them on every level—mental, physical,
emotional, even spiritual. These stories are also peopled with a
supporting cast—family and friends, neighbors and co-workers who
together serve as the community in which your protagonist lives
and loves, providing ample fodder for your main storyline as well
as subplots. These are the characters who give you the room and the
opportunity for your hero to grow, scene by scene and book by book.

Let's take a look at some of the techniques you can use to make your characters resonate with readers—and pull them deeply into your story.

SHAPE-SHIFTING FOR WRITERS

"The characters in my novels are my own unrealized possibilities. That is why I am equally fond of them all and equally horrified by them. Each one has crossed a border that I myself have circumvented." —MILAN KUNDERA

Tana French is a stage actor associated with the PurpleHeart Theatre Company in Dublin, Ireland. Fannie Flagg has appeared on Broadway, on television, and in movies as an actress and comedienne. Maya Angelou was an actress, a singer, and a dancer who toured Europe in *Porgy and Bess* and appeared in the groundbreaking off-Broadway production of Jean Genet's *The Blacks*. James Franco, Tina Fey, Woody Allen, Ethan Hawke, Amy Poehler, Steve Martin, Carrie Fisher, Molly Ringwald, Julie Andrews ... the list of actors who are also successful writers goes on and on. Not to mention the great Bard himself, William Shakespeare.

Writers who create characters readers love (and love to hate) are shape-shifters. Like professional actors, professional writers fully inhabit their characters. They write them from the inside out—and the proof is in the power these charismatic characters hold over readers.

When actors prepare for a role, they go beyond the script. If an actor is playing a surgeon, he observes surgeons in the operating room. If an actress is playing a pregnant teenager, she talks to pregnant teens. When Bradley Cooper played Navy SEAL Chris Kyle in the movie *American Sniper,* he was unable to meet Kyle before he died, so he spent a lot of time with Kyle's father. He gained thirty-five pounds and mastered Kyle's tricky Texan drawl. He even wore the shoes Kyle wore during three tours in Iraq.

writing with quiet hands

You should approach creating a character with the same vigilance. Is your protagonist a beat cop? A physics professor? A pastry chef? Who is your heroine—and what do you know about who she is and what she does?

Good writers, like good actors, do their due diligence. So if your hero is a homicide detective—and you aren't—then interview a real one. People like to talk about what they do. Go for a ride-along; get to know what homicide cops are really like. Then you can write a believable homicide cop, one whom readers will follow happily through your story as she solves crimes and apprehends criminals.

Most of us define ourselves by what we do—and readers admire competency and authenticity.

No matter what your heroine does—and she should do something, as readers now expect characters to have paying jobs, unless they're stay-at-home moms (which is the hardest job of all, she said, having done it herself). If your character is retired, give him volunteer work or a hobby. If she's a teenager, give her obsessions and ambitions and interests. Make an appointment to interview someone who does what your protagonist does—and ask away!

ACTING THE PART

Even if you've never set foot on a stage, you can learn the actor's tricks, tips, and techniques for building a character:

- Take an acting class.
- Make friends with actors, and talk to them about their process. (Actors love to talk about their process.)
- Give your story to actor friends to read, and ask them how they would approach playing the part of your protagonist. What more would they like to know about the character? What would they ask the character if they could? Can you answer those questions?
- Read the classics on acting, which includes this trifecta: *Sanford Meisner on Acting* by Sanford Meisner, *Respect for*

Make Your Hero, Uh, Heroic

Your protagonist should be likable—or at least admirable in some way. We should be willing to pay several dollars for the pleasure of spending several hours in his company.

Give us someone worthy of the title hero. Give us Katniss Everdeen volunteering to take her little sister's place in the Hunger Games. Or James Bond, saving civilization from yet another evil genius. Or young Anne Frank, struggling to stay sane and hopeful in a nightmare world run by grown-ups gone mad with malevolence.

Even if your hero is not so likable, he should be impressive enough in some way to demand our continued attention. Think of Sherlock Holmes, who's smart enough to demand our respect and loyalty. Or the selfish and manipulative Scarlett O'Hara, whose extraordinary survival skills dazzle us through the horrors of the Civil War. Or Dexter, who may be a serial killer, but he's a serial killer whose mission to rid the world of all serial killers is one we can applaud.

Remember Richard Thomas? His protagonist was a man who'd lost everything he cared about and was falling down a rabbit hole to hell. But his hero's journey was so unrelentingly dark, and his actions so increasingly unsympathetic, that the author risked losing his audience. Readers needed to know that however far the hero may have fallen, he would not completely lose his humanity, that there remained a slim hope of redemption. Richard reined in his hero just enough to maintain a shred of his integrity—and I got him a two-book deal.

The most popular heroes are heroic, but they're not perfect. Readers don't like perfect. Because perfect isn't real.

The Devil in You

"Most people carry their demons around with them, buried down deep inside. Writers wrestle their demons to the surface, fling them onto the page, then call them characters." —C.K. WEBB

Think of J.K. Rowling dreaming up Harry Potter, Steig Larsson envisioning Lisbeth Salander, and Jane Austen fancying Mr. Darcy. These are all iconic characters—and all very different from each other as well as from their creators (at least on the surface). Yet they all have demons that their creators have plumbed to good effect. Who knows how the characters' demons relate to those that bedevil their creators ... but it's a safe bet that they do.

We fall in love with these characters because they are so fully realized, so original, and finally, so human. They stand the test of time—and appeal to generations of readers, year in and year out.

A QUESTION OF CRAFT

What are your demons? Make a list of all the things that bedevil you. What tortures you—and how do you torture yourself? Spend at least half an hour considering your inner—and outer—demons. What scares you? What haunts you? What keeps you up at night—and stalks your dreams? This is where the gold is—the private darkness you can mine to create characters who are truly human.

"I am an artisan; I need to work with my hands. I would like to carve my novel in a piece of wood. My characters—I would like to have them heavier, more three-dimensional." —GEORGES SIMENON

The King of Character

Shakespeare wrote the most haunting characters in all of literature: Hamlet, Ophelia, Othello, Iago, Romeo and Juliet, King Lear, Lady Macbeth ... and the list continues. As an actor, Shakespeare played to the audience and created characters who charmed lords and ladies as easily as they charmed the people who bought the penny seats in the pit. His characters are flawed, afflicted with the same fancies and foibles as his fans. And you get the feeling he had fun making them that way.

Which of Shakespeare's characters most resemble those in your work? Reread or watch the plays in which those characters appear. What are their demons? What are your character's demons? How can you use those demons to best effect?

WRITE IT DOWN

Get a pen and some paper, and set the timer for fifteen minutes. Get into character—inhabit your protagonist's body, mind, and spirit. Now write about the one thing you, in your incarnation as your character, would change about your childhood if you could. Write in first person.

Repeat this process for your other lead characters as well.

These exercises are designed to make you think about the forces that have shaped your protagonist. You need to know your heroine inside and out, as well as her past, present, and future. This knowledge will inform your storytelling and drive your heroine's actions and reactions as your story unfolds. But this is not necessarily knowledge the reader needs to know. You're just doing your homework so you can create a well-rounded, proactive protagonist readers will love.

YOUR HERO CHECKLIST

Here's a list of the things you should know about your protagonist:

- age and appearance
- IQ
- physical health
- psychological health
- family history

writing with quiet hands

- formative childhood experiences
- education and career
- character
- core competencies
- relationships
- loves and lusts
- what makes him or her laugh, cry, and fight
- vices and virtues
- motivations and goals
- fears and regrets
- dreams and desires
- obsessions and compulsions

TAKING YOUR BEST SHOTS

"You don't really understand an antagonist until you understand why he's a protagonist in his own version of the world." —JOHN ROGERS

Without the antagonist, the protagonist has nothing to do, no fight to win, no one to defeat. A protagonist without a worthy antagonist is a hero in search of a story. After all, who would Harry Potter be without Lord Voldemort? Or Cinderella without the Wicked Stepmother? Or Sherlock Holmes without Professor Moriarty?

As Clive Barker likes to say, "A story is only as good as its villain." As a storyteller, your job is to create a villain readers love to hate. Consider these worthy antagonists:

- Jeanine Matthews in Veronica Roth's *Divergent*
- Dr. Julius No in Ian Fleming's *Dr. No*
- Cathy Ames in John Steinbeck's *East of Eden*
- Captain Black Jack Randall in Diana Gabaldon's *Outlander*
- Nurse Ratched in Ken Kesey's *One Flew Over the Cuckoo's Nest*
- Hannibal Lecter in Thomas Harris's *Red Dragon*
- Mrs. Coulter in Philip Pullman's *The Golden Compass*

- Captain Hook in J.M. Barrie's *Peter Pan*
- Annie Wilkes in Stephen King's *Misery*
- Edward Hyde in Robert Louis Stevenson's *The Strange Case of Dr. Jekyll and Mr. Hyde*

The right villain can sell your story—and the wrong villain can kill the deal. I have a client whose first thriller was excellent, but the villain of the story was an evil child—and an evil child is a hard sell. Several editors refused to even consider the manuscript because the very thought of a bad-seed kid character made them uncomfortable. Those who did review the manuscript loved the writing but also felt that the young age of the villain made the project too risky for today's tough marketplace.

This story has a happy ending. Undeterred, my client wrote a second novel, this time with an older villain, and I sold it quickly in a two-book deal. (But I may sell that first novel yet. ...)

Here's the lesson: Work as hard on developing your antagonist as you do your protagonist. Make sure she's at least as smart and strong and complex a character as your hero. Don't paint her as all bad; give her a human side that will move readers not to just hate her but rather love to hate her.

DRILL IT DOWN

Play the role of your villain. Write his manifesto. Explain his motivations, dreams, and desires. As you write, remember what actor Tom Hiddleston, who plays Loki, the God of Evil in the *Thor* movie franchise, says about villains: "Every villain is a hero in his own mind."

"A villain must be a thing of power, handled with delicacy and grace. He must be wicked enough to excite our aversion, strong enough to arouse our fear, human enough to awaken some transient gleam of sympathy. We must triumph in his downfall, yet not barbarously nor with contempt, and the close of his career must be in harmony with all its previous development." —AGNES REPPLIER

SPEAKING PARTS

"Each writer is born with a repertory company in his head. Shakespeare has perhaps twenty players. ... I have ten or so, and that's a lot. As you get older, you become more skillful at casting them." —GORE VIDAL

No protagonist is an island; no protagonist stands alone. The most popular heroes are surrounded by friends and foes, neighbors and acquaintances, lovers and spouses, rivals and relatives. This supporting cast serves a number of important storytelling functions. When they are well drawn and well executed, your secondary characters:

- **CREATE THE COMMUNITY IN WHICH YOUR PROTAGONIST OPERATES.** Dorothy lands in Oz, and her new pals the Tin Man, the Scarecrow, and the Cowardly Lion become her community as she tries to make her way to the Wizard.
- **FUEL THE CONFLICT OF YOUR STORY.** Think of Inspector Gamache and the residents of Three Pines, who, one way or another, play into the murder investigations in Louise Penny's popular Chief Inspector Armand Gamache mystery series.
- **CHALLENGE YOUR PROTAGONIST'S IDEAS, ASSUMPTIONS, AND MORALS.** Have you read Gillian Flynn's *Gone Girl*? If you haven't, then you should. Or at least watch the movie—and see the ultimate gauntlet thrown in the world's worst marriage.
- **SERVE AS LEVERAGE, BAIT, OR VICTIMS FOR THE VILLAIN,** as in the *Taken* film franchise, in which Liam Neeson plays Bryan Mills, who's always rescuing his wife and/or daughter.

- **DIVIDE YOUR PROTAGONIST'S LOYALTIES.** This is every cop who must choose between his love of the force, his corrupt fellow cops, and his own integrity—à la Peter Maas's classic biography, *Serpico*.
- **REVEAL YOUR PROTAGONIST IN LOVE AND LUST.** Examples of this abound—from Vladimir Nabokov's *Lolita* and E.L. James's blockbuster *Fifty Shades of Grey* to practically every character in George R.R. Martin's *A Game of Thrones*, with the possible exception of the eunuchs.
- **PROVIDE SUPPORT AND LOYALTY WHEN YOUR HERO MOST NEEDS IT.** Robert B. Parker gave his private detective Spenser a girlfriend—Susan Silverman—and a colleague—Hawk—who do all this for Spenser and more.
- **BETRAY YOUR HERO IN THE WORST POSSIBLE WAYS.** "Et tu, Brute?" says Caesar to Brutus in Shakespeare's *Julius Caesar* as the senators descend upon him. Of course, you can turn this around and make Brutus the hero, whose leader, Caesar, has betrayed him and his Roman republic.
- **SERVE AS MIRRORS FOR YOUR PROTAGONIST.** That's why Elizabeth Bennet has all of those unmarried sisters in Jane Austen's *Pride and Prejudice*; they reflect the limited options available to young women at the time and what can happen when those options work out—or don't.
- **ILLUMINATE YOUR PROTAGONIST'S INNER AND OUTER LIVES.** Many protagonists are misunderstood; they need a best friend to explain them to others—and to themselves. That's why Hamlet had his Horatio and Sherlock Holmes his Dr. Watson and Captain Kirk his Mr. Spock.
- **PUSH YOUR PROTAGONIST TO DO THINGS HE WOULDN'T ORDINARILY DO.** The character who challenges the hero to be more, well, heroic, is often his mentor, such as Luke Skywalker's Obi-Wan in George Lucas's *Star Wars* and Cinderella's Fairy Godmother.
- **PROVIDE (MUCH-NEEDED) COMIC RELIEF.** Many sidekicks serve this purpose, most notably Harry Potter's pal Ron Weasley and Shrek's Donkey.

- **OFFER OPPORTUNITIES FOR NEW STORYLINES AND SUBPLOTS.**
This is true of the majority of series, whose success often depends on the creation of a community of secondary characters to provide enough room for the series to grow. Think of Ed McBain's 87th Precinct series, which set the standard for police procedurals for generations to come.

It Takes a Village

If you're writing a series—and even if you're not—you should work hard to create an interesting supporting cast of secondary characters. A good supporting cast can make the difference between selling your work and not—and that's never been truer than today. Most publishers are looking for projects with series and/or sequel potential—and as we've seen, supporting casts are critical to the success of both.

The digital landscape encourages series publishing because it gives publishers the opportunity to build an author's brand, promote and upsell the author's backlist, and win new readers with every new entry in the series. I've had several clients who thought they'd written stand-alone novels end up with multi-book deals. I even sold one client's stand-alone thriller as Book One in a multi-book deal, with the understanding that Book Two would lend itself to a series. That's why I always advise clients to have ideas for subsequent stories waiting in the wings, so when—and it's almost always when, not if—the editor asks if the project could be a series, we can quickly work up short pitches for those additional books.

From the first book in his best-selling Longmire series, Craig Johnson has surrounded his winning protagonist Walt Longmire, sheriff of Absaroka County, Wyoming—the least populated county in the least populated state—with a strong supporting cast of characters:

- As with most police procedurals, Walt's colleagues at the sheriff's office make up part of his supporting cast: feisty under-sheriff Vic Moretti, receptionist/dispatcher Ruby, and several deputies, including Jim "The Ferg" Ferguson and Turk.

- Walt must also interact with the local officials, including Mayor Steve Brandt; the circuit court judge, Vern Selby; and the prosecuting attorney for the county, Kyle Straub.
- Walt has a grown daughter, Philadelphia lawyer Cady Longmire, and a beloved late wife, Martha, whose death haunts him.
- Dorothy Caldwell runs the Busy Bee restaurant in town, and Ernie Brown runs the local newspaper, the *Durant Courant*. Both characters serve as sources of information and irritation for Walt.
- Walt's best friend, Henry Standing Bear, is from the Cheyenne Nation and runs a local watering hole called the Red Pony.
- Walt's mentor, Lucian Connally, was his predecessor as sheriff.
- The residents and law enforcement officers of the nearby Indian reservation play a key—and sometimes adversarial—role in Walt's investigations.
- Local ranchers, hunters, tourists, and retirees are other groups with whom Walt must deal on a regular basis—not to mention the Division of Criminal Investigation in Cheyenne, the FBI in Washington, and other assorted law enforcement agencies.

You can see how this supporting cast gives Johnson a lot of room in which to stretch for storylines in his novels.

HANDS ON

You might want to create what they call in Hollywood a *series bible* for your story (whether you intend to write a series or a stand-alone novel). You can build it as you research and write. Dedicate pages to your protagonist, antagonist, and secondary characters. Add their family trees, lists of physical and character traits, photos of their houses and cars and clothes, maps of the town they live in, blueprints of their homes and offices. You can also cast your secondary characters with actors you feel would play the roles well; add their photos, too. Fill this series bible with anything and everything you need to create your characters—and capture that

writing with quiet hands

If you're writing genre fiction, then this cast of characters becomes even more important. For science fiction and fantasy writers, creating a strong supporting cast is a critical part of world building (which we'll discuss at length in chapter nine). Readers who prefer police procedurals (and there are millions of them) look forward to getting to know everyone in the precinct, at work, and at home. Women's fiction, by definition, requires a close look at the heroine's relationships with colleagues, friends, and family—especially siblings, parents, and children—and lovers as well. (In fact, if you've written a novel about sisters or mothers and daughters, I'd like to see it. Now.) Cozy mysteries require a small-town setting full of colorful friends and frenemies, and pets, preferably a dog and a cat. Don't laugh—I've had clients who've been asked to add both canines and felines to their novels before the deals were inked.

But no matter what your genre, peopling your work with compelling protagonists, worthy antagonists, and well-rounded secondary characters is key to writing stories that find an audience in today's tough marketplace.

But that's just half the battle. Now you have to step on the gas.

"Believe in your character. Animate (or write) with sincerity." —GLEN KEANE

CHAPTER EIGHT

the engine of narrative thrust

"That's the biggest difference between the BookWorld and the RealWorld ... when things happen after a randomly pointless event, all that follows is simply unintended consequences, not a coherent narrative thrust that propels the story forward." —JASPER FFORDE

As a reader, a writer, and an agent, I read thousands of stories a year— or at least the opening pages of thousands of stories. And, all other things being equal, the reason I most often stop reading is *a lack of narrative thrust*.

Narrative thrust is the taut building of story, beat by beat, scene by scene, chapter by chapter, using the complexities of plot and character to propel the story forward in a dramatic arc that peaks at the climax. You must write each scene so that it leads logically to the next, as if you were connecting a model train, car by car, presenting story questions as you proceed down the track, pushing the action forward to its inevitable, if unpredictable, ending.

GO, STORY, GO!

"Sometimes, a novel is like a train: The first chapter is a comfortable seat in an attractive carriage, and the narrative speeds up. But there are other sorts of trains, and other sorts of novels. They rush by in the dark; passengers framed in the lighted windows are smiling and enjoying themselves." —JANE SMILEY

A lack of narrative thrust occurs when one scene does not logically lead to another. You need to connect each scene, as readers need to know what the protagonist's motives are, and what he wants in every scene. Only then will they care about what happens next. Otherwise your story will read as a series of random scenes strung together—rather than as a compelling narrative.

Narrative thrust provides momentum for a story; it's the gas that fuels your story's engine. You can also think of it as the magnet that pulls the reader through the story. You know it when you experience it—just think of the last story that kept you up all night, the last novel you couldn't read fast enough and yet didn't want to end.

But recognizing narrative thrust as a reader and knowing how to create it as a writer are two very different things. In this chapter, we'll take a look at how you can enhance the narrative thrust of your story—and how you may be unwittingly sabotaging it.

When we talk about novels with narrative thrust, we're not just talking about the page-turners written by the Gillian Flynns and Harlan Cobens of the thriller world. The best novels in every genre boast a strong narrative thrust. Simply put, this means that the authors have mastered the art of the story question—the *who, what, where, when, why,* and *how* questions readers ask themselves as they read, and keep reading.

Much to my family's annoyance, I've been obsessed with story questions since childhood. As a kid, I drove my father crazy asking a million questions as we watched his favorite shows on television. Why doesn't Matt Dillon shoot first (*Gunsmoke*)? Is Captain Kirk going to kill all those cute Tribbles (*Star Trek*)? Can Phelps really train a cat to be a spy (*Mission Impossible*)? Can I be Joey Heatherton when I grow up (*The Dean Martin Show*)? The Colonel, not one to appreciate the artistic temperament, would say in an authoritarian voice, "Watch and find out."

My compulsion to question every beat of a story worsened over time. Once I became a writer and an editor, this obsession became an occupational hazard that always threatened to ruin the viewing pleasure of my nonpublishing friends and family. Yes, I'm the terrible person who leaned toward my companion watching *The Sixth Sense* just a few minutes into the film and stage-whispered, "But he's dead, isn't he?" Even now, decades later, I still drive people crazy by asking questions while we watch a show together. Especially my nonwriter partner, Michael, who, like my father, has a tendency to answer my ubiquitous questions with a sweet if somewhat terse, "Let's watch and find out, honey."

If you do this—aloud or silently—as you enjoy a story in any medium, congratulate yourself. Even if your friends and family hate you for it, it's a good thing. You're thinking like a writer, putting your writing self in the storyteller's place and asking yourself, "What would I do if I were writing this story?" Just as important, you're noticing the story questions in the narrative—and learning by osmosis how you can build them into your own narrative.

Logic *and* Creativity

Personally, I always get a little annoyed when people assume that since I'm a writer, I'm a flake. That is, a person whose imagination trumps her capacity for logic. This misconception has haunted me since my early days in the book business. When I got my first job in book publishing, I was hired as the managing editor on the production side (as opposed to the acquisitions side). Managing editors are by definition deadline-driven powerhouses known for their common-sense toughness, pragmatism, and attention to detail—logical people, in effect. Several years later, when I wanted to move over to acquisitions, I was told by the publisher that I wasn't creative enough to be part of that team. Eventually I overcame this perception and became an acquisitions editor, only to be told a decade down the road by another

writing with quiet hands

publisher, when I wanted to take on a more managerial role, that I was too creative for such a hard-nosed position.

I tell you this story because it illustrates the black-and-white thinking that prevails even in publishing, by people who should know better. The most successful artists balance imagination with craft, creativity with logic. For a writer, this balance is critical because even the most original story told illogically will fail.

When it comes to this delicate balance, narrative thrust is the canary in the coal mine.

You need to build your original story in a sensible way, pulling your readers along clearly and cleanly with story questions that arise logically from your lucid and precise prose.

A QUESTION OF CRAFT

The next time you watch your favorite television show, risk the enmity of your fellow viewers by verbalizing the story questions that occur to you as you watch. If commercials appear during the show, look for the story questions that arise right before each break.

WHAT NOW?

Story questions are posed at the *macro, meso,* and *micro* levels—and your job is to build them all into your prose.

The *macro* story question is the big question that drives the entire plot: Will Cinderella marry her prince? Will Dorothy make it home to Kansas? How will Sherlock Holmes solve the case?

WRITE IT DOWN

Get a pen and some paper, and set a timer for ten minutes. Consider the macro story question of your own work. Write down possibilities and variations; brainstorm. Now narrow it down to one big question: Will my protagonist find true love/ win the war/bring the perpetrator to justice?

Be specific and dramatic. Write down that single macro question, and post it where you can see it as you work on your story. This should help keep your story engine on track.

The *meso* story questions drive each scene: Will Cinderella's stepmother let her go to the ball once she's finished her chores? Will Dorothy survive the cyclone? Will Dr. Watson move into 221B Baker Street with Sherlock Holmes?

And the *micro* questions are the questions scattered through the narrative at every opportunity—the more the better, as shown below.

> Once upon a time there was a gentleman who married, for his second wife [**What happened to the first wife?**], the proudest and most haughty woman that was ever seen [**Why did he marry her? What's wrong with him? Won't she make his life a living hell?**]. She had, by a former husband, two daughters of her own humour and they were indeed exactly like her in all things [**Now there are three of them?**]. He had likewise, by his first wife, a young daughter, but of unparalleled goodness and sweetness of temper, which she took from her mother, who was the best creature in the world [**Uh, oh, what will happen to that poor child now? Will her stepmother favor her own daughters? Will her stepsiblings be nice to her?**].
>
> —from *Cinderella* by Charles Perrault

> The house whirled around two or three times and rose slowly through the air [**Where is the house going?**]. Dorothy felt as if she were going up in a balloon [**What will happen to Dorothy? Will she survive?**].
>
> The north and south winds met where the house stood [**That can't be good, right?**], and made it the exact center of the cyclone [**Is that good or bad?**]. In the middle of a cyclone the air is generally still, but the great pressure of the wind on every side of the house raised it up higher and higher, until it was at the very top of the cyclone [**How high is high? What will happen when the house falls?**]; and there it remained and was carried miles and miles away as easily as you could carry a feather [**What about Dorothy and Toto? What's happening to them? Will they be carried away like feathers, too? When will gravity win out?**].
>
> —from *The Wonderful Wizard of Oz* by L. Frank Baum

Sherlock Holmes seemed delighted at the idea of sharing his rooms with me [**Why would he be delighted when he doesn't even know Watson yet?**]. "I have my eye on a suite in Baker Street," he said [**What's it like? Is a suite big enough for the two of them? Is Baker Street in a good neighborhood?**], "which would suit us down to the ground [**Why would it suit them?**]. You don't mind the smell of strong tobacco, I hope?" [**Will the good doctor want to share a room with someone who smokes?**]

"I always smoke 'ship's' myself," I answered. [**But he's a doctor? Will they both die of lung cancer?**]

"That's good enough. I generally have chemicals about [**What kind of chemicals?**], and occasionally do experiments [**What kind of experiments?**]. Would that annoy you?" [**Why wouldn't it annoy him?**]

"By no means." [**Seriously? Is Dr. Watson the most congenial man who ever lived?**]

"Let me see—what are my other shortcomings [**How many does this guy have?**]. I get in the dumps at times [**Why?**], and don't open my mouth for days on end [**What's wrong with him? Why would he tell Dr. Watson that?**]. You must not think I am sulky when I do that [**Why wouldn't he?**]. Just let me alone [**How can he leave him alone in what might be small quarters?**], and I'll soon be right [**Really? Doesn't this guy need therapy?**]. What have you to confess now? [**Why would Dr. Watson confess any shortcomings to a perfect stranger?**] It's just as well for two fellows to know the worst of one another before they begin to live together." [**Is it really? What will Dr. Watson say?**]

I laughed at this cross-examination. "I keep a bull pup," I said, [**He's a guy with a gun?**] "and I object to rows because my nerves are shaken [**He's a *nervous* guy with a gun? Why doesn't he like to fight?**], and I get up at all sorts of ungodly hours [**Why can't he sleep?**], and I am extremely lazy [**Really? Why would he say that about himself?**]. I have another set of vices when I'm well [**What's wrong with him? Does he have PTSD?**], but those are the principal ones at present." [**Isn't that enough? Is their sharing a flat a nightmare waiting to happen?**]

—from *A Study in Scarlet* by Sir Arthur Conan Doyle

the engine of narrative thrust

117

If you're thinking, *Give me a break, these examples are very old. Times have changed, and the criteria are different now*—well, you're half right. They *are* old examples and times *have* changed and the criteria *are* different—they're even worse now, at least in terms of story questions. You need to start immediately with compelling story questions and keep 'em coming until The Very End, as these recent blockbusters do from the first word:

"We should start back," [**Why should they start back? What's wrong? Where are they? Who are they?**] Gared urged [**Who's Gared? Who's he talking to? Is he scared?**] as the woods began to grow dark around them [**What woods? What comes out when the woods grow dark?**]. "The wildlings are dead." [**What are wildlings? Why are they dead? Did Gared kill them?**]

—from *A Game of Thrones* by George R.R. Martin

Though I often looked for one [**Look for what? Why bother to look?**], I finally had to admit that there could be no cure for Paris [**Why Paris? What cure? Who needs a cure for Paris? What happened to her in Paris? Is she still there? Why does she feel compelled to admit this? What does it mean?**]. Part of it was the war [**Which war? What happened to her in the war? Is the war still raging? Is she in danger? What did Paris have to do with it?**]. The world had ended once already [**Ended how?**] and could again at any moment [**Why? What's going on?**].

—from *The Paris Wife* by Paula McLain

"So now get up." [**Who's talking to whom? Who needs to get up? Who pushed him down? Or did he fall?**]

Felled, dazed, silent, he has fallen [**Who has fallen? Is he badly hurt or just scared? If so, of whom? Did he hit his head? Why is he dazed?**]; knocked full length on the cobbles of the yard [**Cobbles? Yard? Where is he?**]. His head turns sideways; his eyes are turned toward the gate [**What gate? To or from where?**], as if someone might arrive to help him out [**Will someone arrive to help him? Who? Does he have no friends? No family?**]. One blow, properly placed, could kill him now [**Who's going to kill him?**

Whoever's talking to him? Who would want to? Why? What is
he going to do? Just lie there and let it happen?].

—from *Wolf Hall* by Hilary Mantel

Did you note all the story questions raised in just a few opening lines?
That's narrative thrust. That's your competition. That's what you need
to do, too.

DRILL IT DOWN

You've determined your macro story question. Now it's time to
figure out your meso and micro story questions.

1. Go through your scene list (remember your index cards?)
   and write down the story question for each scene. If you
   can't see one, you should rethink that scene; every scene
   needs a strong story question to drive the action forward.
2. Next, go through your story scene by scene, and make
   sure you've peppered your prose with story questions.
   You need at minimum a solid story question every 50–100
   words. More is better.

SCARING READERS SILLY

At its heart, the purpose of narrative thrust is to put the fear of the storytelling gods in your readers. Whether you are writing a horror story or a
lighthearted romance, you are scaring your readers into turning the pages. Do your job right, and they'll want to see what happens next; they'll
need to see what happens next. They'll feel compelled to keep reading,
no matter how late the hour or how long the story.

The logical progression of your scenes, as well as the story questions
that fuel the action in those scenes, are responsible for scaring your readers silly. But just as important is *pacing*, the rate of your narrative thrust.
Pacing is the gait of your storytelling—and a slow horse is a dead horse.

The very word *pacing* has become a touchstone in the industry today;
if I had a dollar for every editor who complained publicly or privately
about the so-called "pacing problems" plaguing today's submissions,

I'd have a lot more dollars—and lot more deals. It's gotten to the point where many editors will refuse to review manuscripts based solely on word counts they deem too high. The rationale: If the story is that long, it must have "pacing problems."

To make sure your pacing is on track, here are some dos and don'ts, all of which you ignore at your peril:

1. **DO** make something happen. The biggest issue in most stories is that not enough happens. There's no narrative thrust without action.

2. **DO** have your protagonist drive that action. The reader wants to identify with the hero, and through him experience the transformative journey that the story takes him on. When the hero is passive or inactive or a bystander to the proceedings, the reader's interest flags.

3. **DON'T** confuse foreshadowing with forecasting. Foreshadowing is a literary tool by which you use tone and style to create a mood or evoke a feeling, typically of foreboding. This helps create suspense. But when you come right out and tell the reader what (usually) bad thing is going to happen, you're forecasting—and eliminating any suspense that may otherwise have strengthened your narrative thrust.

4. **DON'T** break the fourth wall. This is often an excuse to tell the reader what's going to happen before it happens—thereby destroying any suspense you may be trying to build. This is the "If only I had known" device, which is hopelessly old-fashioned and, more often than not, just plain lame. As in: "If only I had known that by the end of the day/night/week/month/year, my career/romance/life would be changed forever." Again, you're depriving your readers of the element of surprise. Worse, you're taking them out of your story to do it.

5. **DO** raise the stakes for your heroine. Give her bigger and bigger obstacles to overcome as your story progresses; make those story questions increasingly challenging.

6. **DO** add a ticking clock if you can. Give your protagonist a hard-stop deadline—if he doesn't find the bomb by 2 P.M., it goes off; if she doesn't tell her mother to butt out of her life by Friday, she'll miss the chance to sail off into the sunset with her beloved on that weekend cruise to Catalina.

7. **DO** as the king of pacing, Lee Child, says: "Write the slow parts fast and the fast parts slow."

8. **DON'T** belabor your descriptions. Stick to the one telling detail. Don't describe your heroine's every feature; just tell us that she never leaves the house without mascara.

9. **DON'T** let your characters talk too much. Dialogue should not replace action.

10. **DO** aim, above all, for clarity. Whenever readers have to stop to think about what you're trying to say—or worse, reread it!—you risk losing them forever.

Pacing is the one element of craft I am very particular about as an agent. If the pacing is off, I won't shop the story. Period.

HANDS ON

Go through your story with Elmore Leonard's directive to "leave out the parts readers skip" foremost in your mind. Whenever you even *suspect* that the narrative thrust is lagging, highlight that section. You'll need to rework it later (with the help of chapters eleven and twelve). Feeling particularly brave? Ask a forthright (nonwriter) friend who's a well-read fan of your genre to read your story and mark wherever he feels bored, lost, or annoyed.

"... there is a tradition of strong narrative thrust in English fiction, and all our great novelists of the past have had it." —P.D. JAMES

CHAPTER NINE

the grounding of setting

"Every story would be another story, and unrecognizable if it took up its characters and plot and happened somewhere else. ... Fiction depends for its life on place. Place is the crossroads of circumstance, the proving ground of, What happened? Who's here? Who's coming? ..." —EUDORA WELTY

The right setting is as important in fiction as it is in real life. Where would Spenser be without Boston? Scarlett O'Hara without Tara? James Joyce without Dublin? Harry Potter without Hogwarts? Raymond Chandler without Los Angeles? Atticus Finch without Maycomb County, Alabama? John Steinbeck without California? Candace Bushnell without New York City?

Only in the right setting can your protagonist bloom where she is planted. It's up to you to plant her in the right place.

I told you earlier about my first writers conference, where I met the marvelous Ray Bradbury. I also met another wonderful writer there, Bill Downey. Bill was a Marine and a World War II veteran who went on to become an acclaimed journalist, author, and teacher at University of California, Santa Barbara, and a fixture at the Santa Barbara Writers Conference. The first African-American reporter hired by the *Santa Barbara News Press*, Bill was a charismatic and big-hearted man who loved writers and writing, and did everything he could to encourage us all to do good work.

Bill was my coach, which meant that he had the dubious pleasure of reading and critiquing the first fifty pages of my lame Nora Ephron–inspired, inanely titled roman à clef, *Hearts and Flowers*, in which a bored, self-deprecating young housewife (*moi*) discovers her husband is having an affair and realizes that she has to do something about her life. Seriously.

The good Mr. Downey was very kind to me. He was one of those writing teachers who believed that praise trumps panning every time. He complimented my oh-so-funny voice and then pointed out, oh-so-kindly, that my work had no setting. No setting at all. Nada. Nichts. Niente. None.

An armchair psychologist would tell you that I forgot setting because, as an Army brat, I'd never lived in any place long enough to know what setting was. And maybe they'd be right. But I know now that lots of writers forget setting, forget to ground each scene in place, forget that when carefully drawn, setting can become a character as real as any person.

I went home happily buoyed by Bill's praise, with a copy of his terrific book on writing, *Right Brain, Write On!: Overcoming Writer's Block and Achieving Your Creative Potential*, tucked in my bag. He'd autographed it for me with the following note: "To Paula, with no question in mind that you'll do well … Bill."

That note got me through a lot of tough times, especially moments when being a writer was the last thing I thought I'd ever be. I still have that book, which occupies a treasured place on my writing bookshelf to this day. Bill died in 1994.

I never forgot setting again.

"I think a setting is hugely important. I look at setting as a character with its own look, sound, history, quirks, goofy temperaments, and moods."
—DEB CALETTI

"WHERE" IS EVERYTHING

If you're like me and have a tendency to forget setting, then you need to make a conscious effort to figure out where everything is in your story. If setting comes more naturally, you still need to be sure that you ground your story in place. As the author, you are the locations scout, the stage manager, the set designer, the props manager, the costume designer, and the dresser. You are the decider of the planet, country, region, county, city, street, *and* building, as well as the room, furniture, and wardrobe of your story.

When you begin a scene, you have to place your players on their stage. You need the equivalent of an establishing shot in filmmaking. With a few quick strokes of the pen you have to do what the camera does in a few seconds. Here are the opening lines of stories by writers of different genres who know how to establish setting quickly, cleanly, and beautifully:

> The man was called Calvin Franz and the helicopter was a Bell 222. Franz had two broken legs, so he had to be loaded on board strapped to a stretcher. Not a difficult maneuver. The Bell was a roomy aircraft, twin-engined, designed for corporate travel and police departments, with space for seven passengers. The rear doors were as big as a panel van's and they opened wide. The middle row of seats had been removed. There was plenty of room for Franz on the floor.
> —from *Bad Luck and Trouble* by Lee Child

writing with quiet hands

Everything about Great Salt Lake is exaggerated—the heat, the cold, the salt, and the brine. It is a landscape so surreal one can never know what it is for certain.

In the past seven years, Great Salt Lake has advanced and retreated. The Bear River Migratory Bird Refuge, devastated by the flood, now begins to heal. Volunteers are beginning to reconstruct the marshes just as I am trying to reconstruct my life.

—from *Refuge* by Terry Tempest Williams

September 2004

Al Tafar, Nineveh Province

The war tried to kill us in the spring. As grass greened the plains of Nineveh and the weather warmed, we patrolled the low-slung hills beyond the cities and towns. We moved over them and through the tall grass on faith, kneading paths into the windswept growth like pioneers.

—from *The Yellow Birds* by Kevin Powers

From her seat in the sanctuary of the Church of the Good Shepherd, Annajane Hudgens wondered if there had ever been a more flawless day for a wedding.

Spring had arrived spectacularly early in Passcoe, North Carolina. Only the first week in April, yet the dogwoods and azaleas were already burst into bloom, and the weeping cherry trees lining the walkway to the church trailed fingertips of pale pink onto a blue and white carpet of violets and alyssum.

—from *Spring Fever* by Mary Kay Andrews

On the afternoon of October 12, 1990, my twin brother Thomas entered the Three Rivers, Connecticut Public Library, retreated to one of the rear study carrels, and prayed to God the sacrifice he was about to commit would be deemed acceptable. Mrs. Theresa Fenneck, the children's librarian, was officially in charge that day because the head librarian was at an all-day meeting in Hartford. She approached my brother and told him he'd have to keep his voice down or leave the library.

—from *I Know This Much Is True* by Wally Lamb

Anyone in the neighborhood could tell you how Michael and Pauline first met.

It happened on a Monday afternoon early in December of 1941. St. Cassian was its usual pokey self that day—a street of narrow East Baltimore row houses, carefully kept little homes intermingled with shops no bigger than small parlors.

—from *The Amateur Marriage* by Anne Tyler

If Walmart is too swank for your taste, maybe a little pricey, you shop at Ocean State Job Lot.

Me and Gus Biletnikov were parked outside one, waiting for a thief to get off work.

Marlborough, Massachusetts. Strip mall on Route 20, a busy east-west road that'll take you all the way across a straight state if you're not in a hurry. The strip mall had grown without any real plan—only locals knew which half-assed access roads led to what. An off-brand supermarket, an off-brand clothing store, a rental center, a good barbeque joint, a CVS.

—from *Shotgun Lullaby* by Steve Ulfelder

In these openings, each writer lays out the scene before us. We envision the scene, we're inside of it—whether it's a battlefield in Iraq or a bird refuge in Utah. Each of these settings is established in about a hundred words, more or less.

Note the specificity of these openings. It's not just any helicopter; it's a Bell 222. Not just any flowers, but dogwoods and azaleas and violets and alyssum. Not just any library, but one found in small-town Connecticut, run by an acting librarian who prefers silence to God. Not just any spring, but a spring that could bring a warrior's death along with it. Not just any marsh, but one threatened by the rising of Great Salt Lake. Not just any neighborhood in Baltimore, but one where you could find love quick before the world came to an end. Not just any strip mall, but one with an Ocean State Job Lot, the poor Massachusetts man's Walmart.

"I use the setting of a small rural Norwegian community—the kind of place that I know so

writing with quiet hands

intimately. I could never write a novel set in a big city, because, frankly, I don't know what it would be like."

—Karin Fossum

Just as these writers have done, think of your story setting as if you were making a movie. Set your stage, place your props, and yell, "Action!"

Specificity is the key here. To be specific, you must pay attention, do your research, and name names. This is hard enough if you know a place well; it's even harder if you do not.

> **WRITE IT DOWN**
>
> Get a pen and some paper, and set the timer for fifteen minutes. Write about the place where you grew up. If you grew up in lots of places, as I did, then pick the one you loved best. Be specific.

PLACE SETTINGS

"I never think of an entire book at once. I always just start with a very small idea. In *Holes*, I just began with the setting; a juvenile correctional facility located in the Texas desert. Then I slowly make up the story and rewrite it several times, and each time I rewrite it, I get new ideas and change the old ideas around." —Louis Sachar

For many writers, like Louis Sachar, setting is the portal by which they can enter the story. They understand that without the right setting, they won't be able to pull off the story they want to tell. Once they find that setting, they can tell their story.

Sometimes it's a happy accident, as we saw with Alice Hoffman, who was inspired to write *The Dovekeepers* after visiting Masada. She hadn't planned on writing that story, but once she'd entered that sacred place, she was compelled to write about it. Other times, a setting from a writer's past haunts him. Think of Kurt Vonnegut, author of *Slaughterhouse-Five*, who was a prisoner of war during the bombing of Dresden, as is his hero, Billy Pilgrim.

And sometimes the setting is simply a place the writer has fallen in love with, as Ernest Hemingway did with Paris. This love affair is recounted in his memoir *A Moveable Feast,* which chronicles his life among American expatriates in 1920s Paris. Based on Hemingway's manuscripts and detailed notes, the book was put together by his wife Mary Hemingway after his death. One of my dearest writer friends, Susan Reynolds, gave me a first edition to celebrate our mutual love of the City of Light, about which Hemingway most famously said: "If you are lucky enough to have lived in Paris as a young man, then wherever you go for the rest of your life, it stays with you, for Paris is a moveable feast." Hemingway names dates and cafés and addresses and people in this wonderful book. I encourage anyone who loves writers and Paris, not necessarily in that order, to read it.

The perfect setting for your story can go a long way to helping you:

- **ESTABLISH YOUR GENRE.** Readers know that any story set on Mars is most likely science fiction (*The Martian Chronicles* by Ray Bradbury), just as stories set in high schools tend to be young adult fiction (*How to Be Popular* by Meg Cabot) and stories set in beach towns are often summer beach reads, a.k.a. women's fiction (*Summer People* by Elin Hilderbrand). This applies to genres that might defy categorization as well. Sarah Addison Allen, who writes a kind of Southern magical realism (as opposed to the Latin American version or what Alice Hoffman calls Yankee magical realism set in New England), believes the South is the perfect setting for her novel *The Sugar Queen*: "Magical realism is a blending of the unusual or supernatural into an otherwise ordinary setting. And, to me, this perfectly describes the South. *The Sugar Queen* involves a lot of magical happenings, but in a very down-home Southern setting. It's full of things that could almost be true."

- **ACHIEVE THE RIGHT TONE.** As we've seen, spooky settings can help you achieve a spooky tone (*The Shining* by Stephen King), just as romantic places can help you achieve a romantic mood (*A Room with a View* by E.M. Forster) and remote settings can help you achieve a feeling of isolation (*Cold Mountain* by Charles Frazier).
- **ENHANCE YOUR STYLE.** Best-selling author Anne Rice sets many of her stories in her native New Orleans, a city rich in history, lush in beauty, and dark in sensuality—all well suited to Rice's own rich, lush, and darkly sensual stories of vampires (*Interview with the Vampire, The Vampire Lestat, The Queen of the Damned*, and more). As Rice says, "I love New Orleans physically. I love the trees and the balmy air and the beautiful days."
- **UNDERLINE YOUR THEMES.** Best-seller author Christopher Moore chose San Francisco as the setting for his hilarious and horrific vampire trilogy—*Bloodsucking Fiends, You Suck,* and *Bite Me*—because, as he puts it: "San Francisco is a breathtakingly beautiful city, with lots of great contrasts between dark and light, often overlapping each other. It's a great setting for a horror story."

Location, Location, Location

The setting you choose may also help set your work apart from the competition—and help you sell it. Setting has played an important role in the success of many of my clients. As we've seen with my client Meera, setting her mystery novel on the Henny Penny Farmette helped her win a series deal. Two of my other writer clients have series that take place on islands—Cynthia Riggs's popular Martha's Vineyard mystery series, the latest of which is *Poison Ivy*, and the aforementioned C. Michele Dorsey's series set on St. John. Another client, James T. Shannon, sets his popular short stories for *Alfred Hitchcock's Mystery Magazine* in his native Fall River, Massachusetts, where he can build stories around the Portuguese-American families he knows so well, including his own. (He's also the author of the novel *Dying for Attention*.)

But perhaps the best examples of setting making all the difference in the careers of my clients concern two very different projects. Shannon Stoker writes science fiction. She set her dystopian trilogy in "an America where girls are breeders and the most beautiful girls go to the highest bidders." Her ability to build out this world made her project *The Registry* an easy pitch for me—and an easy sell.

So, too, for Kim Van Alkemade, who was inspired by the real-life Hebrew Orphan Asylum of Manhattan to write *Orphan #8*, a "moving historical novel about an orphan subjected to experimental X-ray treatments there, who escapes to make a new life for herself, only to face her tormentor years later." Again, an easy pitch for me—and a multi-book deal for Kim.

"I like to know the places I write about. I feel like it helps me ground the novel. My novels are 'realistic novels,' but they can also be fantastical, so it's nice to have a setting that grounds them a little bit."
—JOHN GREEN

DRILL IT DOWN

Many of the most successful stories are all about setting, starting with the title itself:

- *Shutter Island* by Dennis Lehane
- *The House on Mango Street* by Sandra Cisneros
- *Winesburg, Ohio* by Sherwood Anderson
- *Wuthering Heights* by Emily Brontë
- *Brideshead Revisited* by Evelyn Waugh
- *Little House on the Prairie* by Laura Ingalls Wilder
- *Treasure Island* by Robert Louis Stevenson
- *Out of Africa* by Karen Blixen, a.k.a. Isak Dinesen
- *Dune* by Frank Herbert
- *Shanghai Girls* by Lisa See
- *Tobacco Road* by Erskine Caldwell

- *Mansfield Park* by Jane Austen
- *The Magic Mountain* by Thomas Mann
- *Reading Lolita in Tehran* by Azar Nafisi
- *Angel Falls* by Kristin Hannah
- *Cannery Row* by John Steinbeck
- *Miss Peregrine's Home for Peculiar Children* by Ransom Riggs
- *The Red Tent* by Anita Diamant
- *Where the Wild Things Are* by Maurice Sendak

Brainstorm titles for your story based on setting. Come up with ideas related to genre, theme, tone, style, character, familiarity, plot, and more. Which are best suited to your story? How might you exploit what you've learned from this exercise in the writing of your story?

HERE AND NOW, THERE AND THEN

"Obviously, I love to do both contemporary and historical fiction. When a hint of a story grabs me, I try to go with it to see where it will take me, whatever the setting." —KATHERINE PATERSON

Even if you know your story's setting well—it's the city in which you were born and raised, or the university where you got your undergraduate degree, or the beach town where you've summered with your family all your life—you still need to do research. Revisit the places where you set your scenes—and make sure that you can name the streets and alleys, flora and fauna, vehicles and buildings and parks. Best-selling author John Sandford makes a point of going out and looking at the settings he's using in his stories. "If you describe things carefully," says Sandford, "it kind of makes the scene pop."

Be as careful about your smaller stages as your larger ones. If you're setting scenes in places we've seen before—offices and schools and restaurants—find a way to make them unique. I had one client who set scene after scene in his detective novel in diners. Different diners, but diners nonetheless. You need to mix it up.

This is more challenging when your story takes place not in Paris or in an asylum or on a faraway planet but in the "ordinary world" of, say, suburbia. This is where looking for the underbelly—what hides below the surface—can make all the difference. Be sure to scratch your surface and infuse the ordinary with the extraordinary. This is what Chris Van Allsburg, best-selling author and illustrator of such children's classics as *The Polar Express* and *Jumanji*, strives to do in his work. "In the same way that a mundane object can have a personality somehow," says Van Allsburg, "I try to suggest that a mundane setting can have some menace behind it."

Harlan Coben, who has penned a string of best-selling thrillers about ordinary people caught up in extraordinary circumstances, has purposefully chosen the American suburbs for his settings. He doesn't write about worldwide conspiracies that lead to the White House or serial killers stalking mean city streets. Instead he prefers to set his stories in what he calls the "very placid pool of suburbia, family life" where he can "make pretty big splashes." Big splashes, indeed! Coben, one of the most down-to-earth guys you'll ever meet, is a family man whose family man's nightmares fuel his work.

It's hard enough to ground your story in a setting you know well or can visit, but if you're writing historical fiction, science fiction, or fantasy, creating a believable setting is particularly challenging. In the case of historical fiction, you'll need to do your research, to make sure you get the details—from bullets to broomsticks—correct. Because if you don't, even if you're lucky enough to publish your work, warts and all, you'll be hearing about your mistakes from your readers. Over and over again. Even if you're writing science fiction or fantasy, you have to make sure that your setting remains consistent within the context of the world you've created.

But most important, you need to drop your reader into the past or the future or in another country or in another universe without slowing down your story. This is quite a challenge—and one many writers fail to meet. It's one of the biggest—and most common—gaffes writers make, one that will prevent you from selling your work every time. Whenever I critique stories, this problem inevitably comes up. I advise writers to study the work of the masters of world building, who are experts at establishing their settings without affecting the pace. Take a look at the opening chapters of the following works to see how carefully the setting is woven into the tapestry of the story:

- *The Hunger Games* by Suzanne Collins
- *All the Light We Cannot See* by Anthony Doerr
- *A Game of Thrones* by George R.R. Martin
- *The Other Boleyn Girl* by Philippa Gregory
- *Divergent* by Veronica Roth
- *Middlesex* by Jeffrey Eugenides
- *The Martian* by Andy Weir

Note: If you're having trouble integrating world building into your narrative, no worries. We'll discuss how to fix this in greater detail in chapter twelve.

When it comes to setting, you are limited only by your imagination. You can set your story anywhere you'd like. You can send your characters back into the dark recesses of time or fling them far into a future only you can see. You can put them on an island in the Caribbean or on a crater on the moon. You can surround them with French kings and queens or Welsh coal miners and shopkeepers or African zebras and lions. The world of your story is in your hands—and in your hands alone.

"One of the admirable features of British novelists is that they have no scruple about setting their stories in foreign settings with wholly foreign personnel."
—James Buchan

Make It Yours

Setting, like beauty, is in the eye of the beholder. Take New York. Writers have conjured so many versions of New York. In *The Beautiful and Damned*, F. Scott Fitzgerald shows us a Jazz Age New York, peopled with the bored and lost elite of café society. It's a far cry from the New York Betty Smith shows us in *A Tree Grows in Brooklyn*, in which a family struggles to survive in the early years of the twentieth century in the Williamsburg tenements. Then there's Candace Bushnell's *Sex and the City* New York and Edith Wharton's *The House of Mirth* New York and Tom Wolfe's *The Bonfire of the Vanities* New York and Truman Capote's *Breakfast at Tiffany's* New York and Emma McLaughlin's *The Nanny Diaries* New York and Toni Morrison's *Jazz* New York and Chaim Potok's *The Chosen* New York and Kay Thompson's *Eloise* New York and Patti Smith's *Just Kids* New York. How many New Yorks are there? As many as there are writers to write about her.

Whichever setting you choose, be sure to make it yours.

"Setting is my primary joy as a writer, building a world and watching people respond to it."
—NICOLA GRIFFITH

HANDS ON

Make a list of all the settings in your story. Start from the big picture—an astronaut's view—and zoom in slowly. Write a Wikipedia-style entry for the city, town, or county in which your story takes place. *Hint:* If you can't do this off the cuff, you don't know enough about your setting yet.

Next, examine all your scene settings—apartments, airports, strip malls—and figure out how to make them yours.

writing with quiet hands

fun with first drafts

"I hate first drafts, and it never gets easier. People always wonder what kind of superhero power they'd like to have. I want the ability for someone to just open up my brain and take out the entire first draft and lay it down in front of me so I can just focus on the second, third, and fourth drafts." —JUDY BLUME

There are two kinds of writers: those who love writing first drafts and those who hate writing them. Writers who love writing first drafts usually hate editing, otherwise known as subsequent drafts. Those who hate writing first drafts usually love writing the subsequent drafts, because once the dreaded first draft is finished, they have something to edit.

Okay, there are three kinds of writers, if you count the people who hate first drafts *and* subsequent drafts. Why these folks don't just toss their laptops into the Seine and take up investment banking is beyond me. They'd have a lot more fun and almost certainly make more money.

No matter which type you are, you still need to face the blank page and finish your first draft before you can move on to red lining and cutting and pasting those first-draft pages, which are, blessedly, already filled with words, for better or worse.

Note: If you think that you need only one draft, think again. Everyone needs an editor—and you are your own first editor. But we'll talk more about that after we get through the first draft.

THE KITCHEN SINK

"The bottom line is that I like my first drafts to be blind, unconscious, messy efforts; that's what gets me the best material." —JENNIFER EGAN

When it comes to getting that first draft on paper, the only real rule is: whatever works. For some writers, that means outlining every single beat of the story *before* they sit down to write the thing.

When I first started writing long-form works, I never outlined; I wrote my first novel without one. Of course that novel never sold, but it was good enough to get me an agent. It also garnered the attention of an editor who read it and eventually approached me to write a novel for her—but she wanted an outline for that project before she'd give me a contract.

I wrote an outline for her, but it was terrible. Or, at the very least, it was wildly incomplete. Certainly the document I gave the editor was not detailed enough to win me the contract, but I was determined. So I struggled through four more drafts of that outline, refining the story, zooming in closer and closer to the action until I had a scene-by-scene playbook. And then I zoomed in again, writing out the beats of each scene as well. This was an exhausting process; I found it very difficult to build the story brick by brick without actually writing it. But I did it, mostly because I followed my editor's advice: "Go big." By which she meant go for broke in terms of drama.

My editor also strongly advised me to take Robert McKee's Story workshop, the infamous screenwriting seminar immortalized in Spike Jonze's film *Adaptation*. The one and only Charlie Kaufman wrote the screenplay for *Adaptation*, which was inspired by his commission to write a film based on Susan Orlean's bestseller *The Orchid Thief*. Suffering from writer's block, Kaufman ended up writing a hilarious meditation on art, commerce, and the writer in Hollywood instead—turning his humiliating failure to adapt *The Orchid Thief* into cinematic gold. Nicholas Cage, Meryl Streep, and Chris Cooper have a field day in Kaufman's dark romp, which also features Brian Cox as Robert McKee, imperious guru of the commercial script.

When I saw *Adaptation* at a small art film house in Danvers, Massachusetts, I laughed harder than anyone else in the audience—because I was the only one who'd actually *been* to McKee's seminar. Cox nailed McKee. But don't get me wrong: I learned a lot from McKee about structure, writing cinematically, and more, and I always recommend his workshop and *Story*, the book he based on that workshop, to writers. Including you.

Between my editor's crash course in outlining novels and McKee's seminar, I learned what I had to learn about creating a beat-by-beat story structure to write a novel on commission. But like Kaufman, I didn't much like it. And I never did it exactly that way again.

Now my process is more like this: I come up with a concept, a premise, and an opening scene, and I fill my sketchbook with ideas and images and jottings too obtuse to be called real notes. Then I write the first couple of chapters. Fifty pages, tops. By then I have a better sense of where I'm going—and I sit down with my index cards and brainstorm sixty to one hundred scenes. I put them in a loose order, and I start writing. These index cards become, in effect, my outline.

And as I write, I toss in everything but the kitchen sink. Because I know I need to go big, go for broke, pull a Charlie Kaufman. Because I can always edit it later. And I will.

MAKE YOUR OWN RULES: THE PLOTTER

"You have to know what your voice sounds like at the end of the story, because it tells you how to sound when you begin." —JOHN IRVING

In the world according to storytellers, there are plotters and there are pantsers. Plotters revel in writing those beat-by-beat outlines. Plotters use index cards and software programs; they create storyboards and maps and family trees. For a plotter, beginning a novel without a road map would be as unthinkable as driving cross-country without a GPS. And just as stressful.

You may be a *plotter*. You may have to work out the entire story in advance. Many mystery writers do this, figuring out the real story of the murders so they can rework it in a way that misleads the reader. Mystery writers have two storylines to juggle—the one they tell the reader and the one they don't—so plotting it all out beforehand is, for many, a necessity.

Perhaps the ultimate plotter—and one of the best-selling writers in the world—is J.K. Rowling. Rowling spent five years building the world of Harry Potter and plotted out each of the seven books of the series before she wrote the first one. To say her preparation paid off is putting it lightly. We should all be so prepared.

THE PLOTTERS SPEAK

"If I didn't know the ending of a story, I wouldn't begin. I always write my last line, my last paragraph, my last page first."
—Katherine Anne Porter

"I keep an elaborate calendar for my characters detailing on which dates everything happens. I'm constantly revising this as I go along. It gives me the freedom to intricately plot my story, knowing it will at least hold up on a time line."

—Maria Semple

writing with quiet hands

"Normally I start with a plot, and write a synopsis, and the ideas come from the construction."

—Jo Nesbo

"After preliminary research, I zero in on an idea, and then I spend at least four months exploring the topic and in plot building. I jot down every single detail of the plot as bullet points per chapter, and only when the skeleton is complete do I start writing."

—Ashwin Sanghi

"I started as a playwright. Any sort of scriptwriting you do helps you hone your story. You have the same demands of creating a plot, developing relatable characters, and keeping your audience invested in your story. My books are basically structured like three-act plays."

—Suzanne Collins

"I write fast. But it takes me a while to get going. It's very important for me to see my whole plot. I have to see the end first because I like a surprise in the end. Which is why I let characters and plot gestate in my mind."

—Vikas Swarup

"I'm one of those writers who tends to be really good at making outlines and sticking to them. I'm very good at doing that, but I don't like it. It sort of takes a lot of the fun out."

—Neil Gaiman

"I'm a regular guy; I like well-defined outlines. I'm old-fashioned, bourgeois."

—Italo Calvino

"I have a number of writers I work with regularly. I write an outline for a book. The outlines are very specific about what each scene is supposed to accomplish."

—James Patterson

"Due to the sweeping time frame and the voices moving back and forth, the outline for *The Invention of Wings* was the strangest one I've ever done. I created six large, separate outlines, one for each part of the book, and hung them around my study."

—Sue Monk Kidd

"I'm a great believer in outlines."

—Tom Wolfe

"I start with a beat sheet, which is more of an abbreviated outline. It hits all the major plot points. From there, I move to note cards. But the most important part of my process is my inspiration board."

—Kami Garcia

"Characters are incredibly important, but I tend to build them around the plot during the outline stage. However, once I'm writing the manuscript, the characters I'm writing dictate how the plot unfolds."

—Aimee Carter

But you don't have to be a mystery writer to be a plotter. Perhaps, like John Irving, you can't write the beginning until you've determined the ending. Irving claims to write his best-selling novels in reverse, writing the last line first and then writing the line before that, working backwards for a while, until he truly understands the ending.

For plotters, knowing where the story is going in advance frees them to write that story with abandon. If you are the sort of person who likes to make lists, plan your vacations ahead of time, and buy your Christmas presents year round, you may be a plotter.

The good news: Agents and editors will love you because you'll be able to provide the synopses they need to contract the stories you haven't written yet.

WRITE IT DOWN

Get a pen and some paper, and set a timer for fifteen minutes. Write down all you know—or suspect you know—about your plot at this very moment.

writing with quiet hands

Be Prepared to Plot

As your career moves forward, the ability to create and write to an outline becomes increasingly important. I have a client whose first novel I sold in record time in a substantial multi-book deal. Like most first-time novelists, she'd had years to write this first book, but now she was faced with producing two more novels in her science fiction series on an accelerated schedule. She had only nine months to write each subsequent story. She had ideas for these two books, which I'd pitched as part of the deal, but these short blurbs were all she had. She hadn't outlined the first novel; she had just winged it. She wrote the second book, winging it as well.

Second novels can be challenging to write, given the pressure and the time constraints, neither of which the writer has had to deal with before. This "second-book syndrome" makes editors—and writers— nervous, with good reason. The publishing landscape is littered with the careers of novelists whose second books have failed. The critics seem to have it out for second books, whose reviews are often less than stellar, if not outright pans. That said, the criticism can be deserved, because the writer chokes and the book is not as good as it should be.

Second-book syndrome can hit creators of trilogies particularly hard. The middle book of any trilogy can be notoriously tough to write. Middle stories are in effect the second acts of the trilogy, and like the second acts of individual stories, they can be problematic. They have to build on the promise of the first book, set up the action for the climax of the last book, and still be entertaining and engaging enough to stand on their own. Science fiction and fantasy writers must also live with the world-building choices they made in the first book. Consistency is key.

For my client, the second book proved a struggle. The editor wanted a lot of structural changes. She wrote a second draft of the second book, but the editor was still not satisfied and called me in to help. We brainstormed a new structure for the novel, and my client created a new outline for the second book. She rewrote it quickly, and the book was recently published on schedule. I'm happy to report that the novel has now been nominated for a major literary award—a rare achievement for the middle book of a trilogy.

I tell you this story because even if you are a pantser, there may come a time in your career when you need to think like a plotter, like it or not.

NO RULES, NO WORRIES: THE PANTSER

"I am a hopeless pantser, so I don't do much outlining. A thought will occur to me, and I'll just throw it into the story. I tell myself I'll worry about untangling it later. I'm glad no one sees my first drafts except for my poor editor and agent." —MARIE LU

If you resist rules, including your own, you may be a pantser. You just sit down and write, making up the story as you go along—by the seat of your pants, as it were. You proceed in good faith, confident that whatever happens, you'll make it work. And most of the time you probably will.

If you are a pantser, you're in good company. A surprising number of best-selling writers do not outline. Even those writers who create big series and complicated worlds often eschew plotting in advance of the writing—including the likes of George R.R. Martin and Diana Gabaldon. Many mystery writers, for whom tightly plotted stories are a genre requirement, also do not plot. I did an informal survey of a few of my mystery-writing friends and clients who do not plot—and count Hank Phillippi Ryan, Hallie Ephron, James D. Shannon, Dick Cass, and Michele Dorsey among them. (They all claim that my book *Plot Perfect* is converting them—but I'm not sure I believe that.)

Storytellers who write character-driven stories may place their characters on the stage—and then let them improvise their way through the story. Some writers simply begin with a given situation, put their characters in that situation, and let 'er rip. This approach can work very well for these writers, particularly those with high-concept stories. Other writers simply daydream their way through their stories.

If you're a pantser, then pants away. But do it with the understanding that sometimes you will pants yourself right into corners or begin stories that you simply cannot finish. We've all heard about the novels that writers abandoned when they realized halfway or more into the story that the book was simply going nowhere—and there was no saving it. Most pantsers have at least one abandoned novel in a drawer somewhere.

DRILL IT DOWN

Write a scene as a pantser, completely unscripted. Do as Siegfried Lenz does: Just sit down in front of a window and wait for a plot to "rise slowly" in your mind. Now write it down. What about this pantser process appeals to you? What doesn't? How long does it take? How does it compare to your usual process?

THE PANTSERS SPEAK

"If I had a plot that was all set in advance, why would I want to go through the agony of writing the novel? A novel is a kind of exploration and discovery, for me at any rate."
—Chaim Potok

"As a matter of writing philosophy, if there is one, I try not to ever plot a story. I try to write it from the character's point of view and see where it goes."
—Andre Dubus III

"I don't plot the books out ahead of time. I don't plan them. I don't begin at the beginning and end at the end. I don't work with an outline, and I don't work in a straight line."
—Diana Gabaldon

"Many writers will get a contract by selling chapters and outlines or something like that. I wrote the entire novel, and when it was all finished, I would give it to my agent and say, 'Well, here's a novel; sell it if you can.' And they would do that, and it was good because I never had anyone looking over my shoulder."

—George R.R. Martin

"I've often wished when I started a book I knew what was going to happen. I talked to writers who write eighty-page outlines, and I'm just in awe of that."

—Charlaine Harris

"I don't plan. I don't outline. I have hated outlines since sixth grade. ... I just like to see where the story goes."

—J.A. Jance

"I don't like plots. I don't know what a plot means. I can't stand the idea of anything that starts in the beginning, you know, 'beginning, middle, and end.'"

—Maira Kalman

"I write sentence to sentence. That's the kind of writer I am. I don't have a plot when I begin. I have to be convinced, and I have to be surprised."

—Lorraine Adams

"In writing, I'm totally anti plans of any kind. All my attempts to plan and plot novels have come to grief, and in expensive ways."

—Peter Temple

"Quite casually I wander into my plot, poke around with my characters for a while, then amble off, leaving no moral proved and no reader improved."

—Thorne Smith

THE HAPPY MEDIUM: THE PLANTSERS

Best-selling author Claire Cook, one of my favorite people and a role model for maneuvering through the new publishing landscape, says that pantsers and plotters have more in common than you might think.

writing with quiet hands

Most plotters acknowledge that sticking too closely to an outline, however well detailed, may keep them from recognizing and capitalizing on the happy accidents that can occur along the writing journey and bring a story to life. Staying open to such unexpected developments is critical; surprising yourself means surprising the reader, to paraphrase Robert Frost. On the other hand, most pantsers admit that at a certain point, they need to stop, take a step back, and look at the story as a whole, reviewing where they've been and where they're going.

Both approaches to the first draft—plotting and pantsing—are valid; each has its admirers and detractors. But in the end, or by the end, as the case may be, you may find that a combination of both methods is what best gets you through that first draft. Which would make you what my client Kate Defrise, author of such delightful novels as *Christmas Chocolat,* calls a "plantser." Well, first she said "plonsters," unaware of the little monsters on the children's TV show *Plonsters.* So we changed it to plantsers, which I like even better because it implies a certain organic growth.

THE PLANTSERS SPEAK

"I just focus on getting the first scene right, with a few lines about the overall plot, and then the book grows organically."
—Alexander McCall Smith

"Before I start, I trick myself into thinking I know what's going to happen in the story, but the characters have ideas of their own, and I always go with the characters' choices. Most of the time I discover plot twists and directions that are better than what I originally had planned."
—Neal Shusterman

"I plot the first five or six chapters quite minutely, and also the end. So I know where I am going but not how I'm going to get there, which gives characters the chance to

develop organically, as happens in real life as you get to
know a person."

—Joanna Trollope

"I outline in some detail, but even after the outline is done
I often get a new idea that is an improvement, so the
outline is a living, breathing thing as well. I also re-outline
when I'm two-thirds done, to be sure that there is an
emotional payoff from all the plotlines and to be sure the
story is as tight as it can be."

—Jeff Abbott

THE FINISH LINE

"I prefer to write first drafts as soon as possible after
waking so that the oneiric inscape is still present to
me." —WILL SELF

The most important rules for writing a first draft are these:

1. Whatever works.
2. It takes as long as it takes.

Whatever you have to do to get through your first draft, do it. Plot
it—or not. Pants it—or not. Follow a trail of index cards, or pour out
your story on the page willy-nilly. Write your first draft in longhand
on yellow legal pads at dawn before work, or dictate it into your smart-
phone on your commute, or type it on your laptop every evening after
the ten o'clock news.

Whatever works. The trick is to get the story down, from beginning to end. Because the people who get published are those who:
(1) finish and (2) revise. Finish your first draft and you are halfway there.

When I wrote my first book, I realized that I couldn't write it in
one long spurt. As a journalist, that's how I'd written my longest stories; I'd sit down with all of my research and interview notes and
pound out the story in one extended session. But I couldn't write a
book in a day or a night or even a long weekend. I had to learn to break

up my story into chapters and scenes and beats, and commit to finishing at least one a day until I reached the end.

Writing a book is a marathon, not a sprint. If you're a sprinter, then you'll need to master some of the marathoner's tricks before you set out on your journey. Otherwise you will hit the wall and fail to cross the finish line. Here are some strategies that might help:

- **WRITE EVERY DAY.** Every day. You need to stay in the story; if you stand apart from it for too long you will find it hard to get back into the rhythm again.
- **WRITE AT THE SAME TIME EVERY DAY.** This way you'll train yourself to return to your story at the stroke of 10 P.M., or when your alarm rings at 6 A.M., or when your kids go to bed at 8:30 P.M.
- **END YOUR WRITING SESSION WHILE YOU'RE ON A ROLL.** This was a trick Ernest Hemingway used; he believed that you should stop for the day "when you are going good and when you know what will happen next." That way, you can slip back into your story the next day.
- **REWARD YOURSELF WHEN YOU MEET A BENCHMARK.** If you are the sort of person who responds well to rewards—chocolate, concert tickets, new shoes/skis/suits—then build rewards into your writing schedule. As I write this chapter, I'm propelled by the prospect of my next reward—dinner and a movie with a writer friend whose book deadline is the same day as mine. Every 10,000 words, we take what Julia Cameron calls "an artist's date" together. (More about these in chapter fourteen.) It's fun—and it works.
- **GIVE YOURSELF A WRITING VACATION.** Sometimes you need time away from work, family, friends, and the distractions of home to get traction on your story. Go. Alone. Write.

I'd been working on my first novel for years and found myself engaged to a very nice man before I managed to complete the first draft. I was determined not to get married before I finished it. So I checked myself into the Sylvia Beach Hotel in Nye Beach, Oregon, for a week. Named after the beloved patroness of the arts who opened the famous Shakespeare & Company bookstore in Paris, this beachside landmark bills itself as "truly a hotel for book lovers," and it is. Rooms are named after and have décor inspired by specific writers; I stayed in the Alice Walker room and the Willa Cather room. There are no phones or TVs or Wi-Fi in the rooms, but there are books everywhere, and the top floor is a library with overstuffed chairs that overlooks the Pacific Ocean. I finished my first draft there and married that very nice man three months later.

When none of these strategies work, and you find yourself staring out the window and not writing, or writing words that don't seem to lead anywhere, or getting lost in your story with no way out, just keep showing up and writing. As my friend Rob told me, it's all part of the process. When Rob wrote his first novel, he spent a year at his desk starting stories that went nowhere, until he realized that he was just finding his way into the story. He didn't know how to write a novel—it was his first one—and he was figuring out how to do it. "All those fits and starts," he told me, "were all the same novel. I just didn't know it."

HANDS ON

Write the first draft of something: a song, a poem, a short story, an essay, a scene, a chapter. Get used to finishing things. Be the kind of writer who finishes what you start. Revel in the satisfaction that comes with completion. Repeat. Repeat. Repeat.

"I am violently untidy. My desk is overcrowded. I write my first drafts in longhand in a long notebook using a plastic throwaway fountain pen. Then I work on a word processor using a different desk and a different room." —COLM TÓIBÍN

CHAPTER ELEVEN

the second-draft deep dive

"My only writing ritual is to shave my head bald between writing the first and second drafts of a book. If I can throw away all my hair, then I have the freedom to trash any part of the book on the next rewrite." —CHUCK PALAHNIUK

Don't panic, you don't have to shave your head to celebrate the commencement of your second draft. But there is a certain poignancy in Chuck Palahniuk's willingness to do so. The best-selling author of *Fight Club* makes a good point about preparing yourself for the deep dive of the second draft. Short of cutting off all your hair, here are some strategies you might want to consider when preparing for your own second draft.

1. **PUT THE MANUSCRIPT ASIDE FOR A WHILE.** One week is good; one month is better. The more distance you put between the first draft and the second, the more clear-eyed you'll be when it's time to get started. Try not to think about the story during this time; jot down notes when you must, but consider going on vacation or indulging in other interests or getting back in the social swing of

things or doing any activity you may have neglected while focused on pounding out that first draft.

2. **FIND SOME BETA READERS.** Many writers swear by this process. It might work well for you, too, depending on who your beta readers are, the kind of feedback they give you, and how well you handle and process criticism. If you have an agent, he may be your first-draft reader. Or maybe it's your wife or your writing group or an editor you commission to read and comment on your work. If you have a contract, you may be tempted to send your first draft directly to your acquisitions editor, that is, the editor who bought your book. Resist that impulse. As a general rule, take the feedback you get from amateurs with a grain of salt—they don't know any more than you do. Take the feedback from professionals—agents, editors, and published writers in your genre—seriously. Just remember that while they may be right about the issues you need to address, they can be way off in terms of how to address those issues. If you find that you are simply not ready to show anyone your work yet, or you tend to choke when you get too much feedback too early, then don't.

Whatever you do, you need to approach this second draft with a seriousness of purpose, just as Palahniuk does. Remember, the people who get published are the writers who (1) finish and (2) revise. The good news is, you've finished. Now you can revise. This process is a lot like making dessert. When you're writing your first draft, you know you're making dessert, but you won't know until you finish if you've made a pie or a cake. Now that you know it's a cake, you can go back through and make your dessert more cakelike—through revision.

This second-draft revision is not the same as copyediting or line editing. (More on those later.) Most writers can figure out—or hire out—the copyediting and line editing they need. But such editing would be premature at this point—that's icing on the cake—so don't waste your time or money by soliciting those services too soon. Too many writers jump right from first draft to line editing or copyediting—and miss the most important edit of all, the one that can make the difference between success and failure.

What you're doing now, at the second-draft stage, is a kind of supercharged developmental edit, in which you:

- identify the themes and weave them through the story.
- look at the imagery and symbology of your story.
- milk the drama—that is, figure out what works and doesn't work in your story in terms of structure, character, and point of view.

This supercharged developmental edit is what can make the difference between getting published and not getting published, and can help you find and keep an audience and/or write that breakout book if you've been languishing in the midlist ranks.

I have a client who's a very good writer, whose mystery novels always placed in the top three of the St. Martin's Minotaur/Malice Domestic Mystery writing contest, one of the leading competitions in the genre. But she never won and she never revised and she never got a book contract; she just kept on writing novels. Not because she was lazy or inept or resisted revision, but because she had written up to her current level of craft and didn't know how to get to the next level.

When I found out that she'd done so swell in these contests, I immediately asked to read one of the manuscripts and discovered that she was doing a lot right; she created strong plots and compelling characters and she had an engaging voice. But she'd made some of the mistakes that editors don't want to take on, and was missing a level of refinement that comes only with a strong second-draft revision. I gave her notes, and she revised, and revised again, and bingo! I got her a multi-book deal—and the first book in her new series will be out later this year.

You can hire a developmental editor to give you this kind of feedback, but before you do, try to do as much of a second-draft deep dive as you can by yourself. Let's take a look at the elements you should focus on during this revision.

A QUESTION OF CRAFT

Where are you in terms of craft? What do your own instincts—and/or the feedback from other writers and publishing professionals—tell you?

THEME WEAVER

"Ultimately, your theme will find you. You don't have to go looking for it." —RICHARD RUSSO

As Richard Russo points out, quite rightly, your themes should find you. Now that you've written your first draft, you should be able to determine what you're really writing about. You thought you were writing a love story, but what you're really writing about is loss—and how love can help people survive life's inevitable losses. Or you thought you were writing a high-concept, plot-driven thriller, but what you're really writing about is revenge—and how the need for vengeance can drive even the most ordinary man to extraordinary deeds. Or you thought you were writing a family saga, but what you're really writing about is the sins of the fathers—and how those sins can revisit every generation.

You may have to look no further than your own experiences and obsessions. Most of us writers write about what scares us, consumes us, amuses us, comforts us, and/or bedevils us. As Stephen King likes to tell people who ask him why he writes what he writes: "What makes you think I have a choice?"

Charles Dickens was driven by his passion for the underdog, and his stories—*Oliver Twist, Nicholas Nickleby, Bleak House*, and so forth—dramatize the economic, social, and moral injustices of Victorian life. This passion sprang from his childhood, during which his father was sent to debtor's prison and Dickens was forced at the tender age of twelve to work in a shoe-blacking factory. Leon Uris dedicated much of his oeuvre—*Exodus, QB, Mila 18, QB VII*—to fighting anti-Semitism after the Holocaust. Uris was a Jewish American who served as a U.S.

Marine in the South Pacific during World War II. Maya Angelou drew upon her own life to explore the themes of feminism, racism, child abuse, identity, and family in her acclaimed autobiographical works of poetry, essays, plays, songs, and memoirs, including *I Know Why the Caged Bird Sings.* Anne Rice wrote the groundbreaking *Interview with the Vampire* after her young daughter died from leukemia, a blood disease. As we've seen, Janwillem Van de Wetering drew the themes for his police procedurals from his time as a cop and his Buddhist practice.

If you're thinking that your life has been way too ordinary to serve as the seeding ground for such mighty themes, think again. Claire Cook, best-selling author of such novels as *Must Love Dogs*, sees her major theme as reinvention. Her novels have all been about people who must reinvent themselves to survive—and thrive. Cook reinvented herself as an acclaimed novelist at midlife and now has become a reinvention guru of sorts, speaking at conferences and running workshops on the subject. Her recent book, *Never Too Late*, is not a novel but rather a self-help treatise on reinvention (and has some great tips about making a name for yourself as a writer).

Ultimately, private preoccupations fuel our work and provide us with themes, like it or not.

Sit down with your story and identify your themes. If you've used beta readers, ask them what they think your story is really about. Explore the emotions that drive your characters. That's where the juice of theme is. Once you know your theme, ask yourself what metaphor you're using—or can use—to underscore it.

"My world view is that it can all go to hell in an instant, and you have to be ready for it. That's pretty much the central theme running through my work. It's about people's awareness of how uncertain life can be and their trying to guard against that."
—DAVID MORRELL

Get a pen and some paper, and set the timer for twenty minutes. Write down whatever personal experiences, obsessions, nightmares, demons, and/or desires haunt you. How do they inform your first draft? How might they help you enhance your second draft?

CREATING AN IMAGE SYSTEM

"For myself, the only way I know how to make a book is to construct it like a collage: a bit of dialogue here, a scrap of narrative, an isolated description of a common object, an elaborate running metaphor which threads between the sequences and holds different narrative lines together."
—HILARY MANTEL

Metaphor is the lifeblood of storytelling. Finding the metaphor for your story—and capitalizing on it in your second draft—is a concrete way to take your work to the next level. Find the metaphor, and you can build an image system around it and perhaps add an organizing principle as well. Let's take a look at the definitions of these terms:

A *metaphor* is a symbol or image used to represent something else. For a storyteller, stories are metaphors for life.

An *image system* is the collection of recurring patterns and motifs in a story. The best image systems relate to the theme and metaphor of the story.

An *organizing principle* is the conceptual framework for a story. Diaries, journals, blogs, units of time, instructions, transcripts—all these and more can be used as organizing principles for a story.

Metaphors, image systems, and organizing principles are the refinements that can mark well-crafted work. Here are some examples:

THE SECRET LIFE OF BEES BY SUE MONK KIDD

METAPHOR: The hive and bees serve as a metaphor for life/community, as led by the queen bee.

IMAGE SYSTEM: bees, honey, the hive, the sacred feminine

ORGANIZING PRINCIPLE: Each chapter opens with a snippet from *The Beekeeper's Manual.*

MY HORIZONTAL LIFE: A COLLECTION OF ONE-NIGHT STANDS BY CHELSEA HANDLER

METAPHOR: The author uses sex as a metaphor for love and relationships and even of life itself.

IMAGE SYSTEM: sexual imagery and language

ORGANIZING PRINCIPLE: The author's life is told in a series of one-night stands.

A GAME OF THRONES BY GEORGE R.R. MARTIN

METAPHOR: In this story, life is presented as a fight to the death through the metaphors of war and the struggle for power.

IMAGE SYSTEM: winter, snow, ice, wolves, cold, knives, axes, swords

ORGANIZING PRINCIPLE: The story is a fantastical retelling of the War of the Roses, organized by the points of view of the main characters.

THE YEAR OF LIVING BIBLICALLY: ONE MAN'S HUMBLE QUEST TO FOLLOW THE BIBLE AS LITERALLY AS POSSIBLE BY A.J. JACOBS

METAPHOR: The author uses the Bible as a metaphor for a good life as he strives to live according to its directives.

IMAGE SYSTEM: biblical motifs and language

ORGANIZING PRINCIPLE: The author describes 365 days of living a literal interpretation of the Bible.

LIKE WATER FOR CHOCOLATE: A NOVEL IN MONTHLY INSTALLMENTS WITH RECIPES, ROMANCES AND HOME REMEDIES BY LAURA ESQUIVEL

METAPHOR: In this magical realism novel, food is used as a metaphor for life.

IMAGE SYSTEM: food, cooking, fire
ORGANIZING PRINCIPLE: The subtitle says it all.

Many stories are built around the metaphor of a journey—that is, life as a journey. Let's take a look at two different journey stories.

Eat, Pray, Love by Elizabeth Gilbert

In *Eat, Pray, Love,* Elizabeth Gilbert's best-selling memoir of self-actu-alization, a depressed American divorcee goes on a journey in search of the meaning of life—only to find herself. Gilbert needs to learn to nurture herself, and she does so in three acts. In Act One, she learns to feed her body by eating in Italy; in Act Two, she learns to feed her soul by praying in India; and in Act Three, she learns to feed her heart by falling in love in Bali.

Each act has its own image system, as revealed in the prose itself.

- The pasta and libations and linguistic pleasures of Italy:

  Plastic red-checkered tablecloths. Homemade *limoncello* liqueur. Homemade red wine. Pasta served in unbelievable quantities by what Luca calls "little Julius Caesars"—proud, pushy, local guys with hair on the backs of their hands and passionately tended pompadours.

- The ashram and chanting and meditation of India:

  But when I try to go to the chant, all it does is agitate me. I mean, physically. I don't feel like I'm singing it so much as being dragged behind it. It makes me sweat. ... Everyone else sits in the chant hud-dled in wool blankets and hats to stay warm, and I'm peeling layers off myself as the hymn drones on, foaming like an overworked farm-horse. I come out of the temple after the Gurugita and the sweat rises off my skin in the cold morning air like fog ... .

- The gurus and temples and expats of Bali:

  Weird things happen in the evenings. We stumble upon mysterious temple rituals in the middle of nowhere, let ourselves get hypnotized by the chorus of voices, drums and gamelan.

Gilbert strings 108 transformative experiences together in a *japa mala,* the traditional prayer beads of India (on which the rosary is based). The *japa mala* is her organizing principle.

The Unlikely Pilgrimage of Harold Fry
by Rachel Joyce

In this charming and moving novel, Harold Fry, a bored and boring retired brewery manager from Devon, goes to mail a letter to his ailing friend Queenie and keeps on walking—right past the post office and all the way up the length of England, a total of 647 miles—in the hope of saving her life. The story recalls both John Bunyan's *The Pilgrim's Progress* and Chaucer's *The Canterbury Tales* and is similarly organized, complete with the cast of colorful characters Harold meets along the way.

Joyce tells the story mile by mile, encounter by encounter, and revelation by revelation, as the colorless Harold trudges on toward his dying friend. As he walks, Harold warms to the natural beauty of the English countryside, opens his heart to the people he meets, and remembers how much he loves his wife—and life itself.

> Life was very different when you walked through it. Between gaps in the banks, the land rolled up and down, carved into chequered fields, and lined with ridges of hedging and trees. He had to stop to look. There were so many shades of green Harold was humbled.

The sea—where Harold's journey begins and ends—plays an important role in the image system of the novel, as does the landscape of England, home, and heart.

> The pewter sea lay behind, while ahead of him was all the land that led to Berwick, where once again there would be sea. He had started; and in doing so Harold could already see the end.

"Borges said there are only four stories to tell: a love story between two people, a love story between three people, the struggle for power, and the voyage. All of us writers rewrite these same stories ad infinitum." —PAULO COELHO

Consider the journey stories below. Choose one you know and have read, or one you'd like to read or reread. Consider how the author uses the metaphor of the journey to tell the story. What is the image system? Is there an organizing principle?

- *Wild* by Cheryl Strayed
- *Alice's Adventures in Wonderland* by Lewis Carroll
- *The Adventures of Huckleberry Finn* by Mark Twain
- *The Road* by Cormac McCarthy
- *The Left Hand of Darkness* by Ursula K. Le Guin
- *The Odyssey* by Homer
- *The Alchemist* by Paulo Coelho
- *Ladder of Years* by Anne Tyler
- *On the Road* by Jack Kerouac
- *The Girl in the Road* by Monica Byrne
- *Heart of Darkness* by Joseph Conrad
- *A Year by the Sea* by Joan Anderson
- *The Wonderful Wizard of Oz* by L. Frank Baum
- *Journey to the Center of the Earth* by Jules Verne

WRITERS ON METAPHOR

"I know that I'm going to die and that you're going to die. I can't do anything about that. But I can explore it through a metaphor and make a kind of funny, dark story about it, and in doing so, really exhaust and research as many aspects of it as I can imagine. And in a way, that does give me some closure."

—Chuck Palahniuk, author of *Fight Club*

"I think zombies have always been an easy metaphor for hard times. Because they're this big, faceless, brainless group of evil things that will work tirelessly to destroy you and think of nothing else."

—Seth Grahame-Smith,
author of *Pride and Prejudice and Zombies*

"Most people like to read about intrigue and spies. I hope to provide a metaphor for the average reader's daily life. Most of us live in a slightly conspiratorial relationship with our employer and perhaps with our marriage."

—John le Carré,
author of *Tinker, Tailor, Soldier, Spy*

"In literature, the ghost is almost always a metaphor for the weight of the past. I don't believe in them in the traditional sense."

—Tabitha King, co-author of *Candles Burning*

"I always thought of vampires, especially the young adult ones, as a metaphor for sex—sucking blood, forbidden, taboo. I think they just ooze sex. Vampires are all the big themes in life in one attractive, bloodsucking package."

—Melissa de la Cruz, *Vampires of Manhattan*

"I've spoken often of how the fantasy genre is able to, with the greatest freedom among all the genres, take a metaphor and make it real. But of course that's only the starting point."

—Steven Erikson, author of the
Malazan Book of the Fallen series

"Quest is at the heart of what I do—the holy grail, and the terror that you'll never find it, seemed a perfect metaphor for life."

—Jeanette Winterson,
author of *Oranges Are Not the Only Fruit*

"Of course I didn't pioneer the use of food in fiction: It has been a standard literary device since Chaucer and Rabelais, who used food wonderfully as a metaphor for sensuality."

—Joanne Harris, author of *Chocolat*

> "My father died when I was seven. I guess I am interested in fatherlessness as a metaphor for vulnerability and unprotectedness. Being on your own in the world in a way you're not quite ready for, ever."
> —Mary Gordon, author of *The Shadow Man*

> "I discovered that the horse is life itself, a metaphor but also an example of life's mystery and unpredictability, of life's generosity and beauty, a worthy object of repeated and ever-changing contemplation."
> —Jane Smiley, author of *Horse Heaven*

Ray Bradbury credited his success as a writer to his strong sense of metaphor. As you go through your revision, find ways to strengthen the metaphor of your story. Consider the image system that may complement your metaphor; look for the patterns and motifs that appear in your work and expand on them. If you think you may be able to employ an organizing principle, use it as a framework. Your story will be better for it.

MILKING THE DRAMA

"I think remarkable storytelling always finds an audience." —JEFF BEZOS

The purpose of the second-draft deep dive is to find the remarkable storytelling in your first draft—and milk it. In my experience, one of the most common reasons editors pass on a story is a lack of drama. Even a manuscript riddled with other problems may interest a publisher if the potential for drama is present. So now that you have your first draft on paper, you need to ask three questions:

- Who's telling the story?
- What happens in the story?
- Who makes it happen?

Who's Telling the Story?

Simply put, who's telling the story is determined by the chosen point of view. Generally the protagonist should tell the story. Why? *Because it's the protagonist's story.* Readers want to know what the hero is thinking and feeling; they want in on his inner life.

Deprive readers of your heroine's innermost thoughts and feelings, and you'll lose those readers. The inner life is the novel's last best defense against all of the other activities that compete for the reader's attention—from television, theater, and film to video games, the Internet, and social media. Only fiction (and creative nonfiction) lets readers into the head of the hero, where they can hear his thoughts as he thinks them; other media show us what the hero does and says, but deny access to his inner life (apart from the occasional lame voice-over).

That's why you need to make sure that most—if not all—of your story is told from your protagonist's point of view. She is who your readers are supposed to care about, the person they need to fall in love with, the person they'll follow through three hundred or more pages. While there is room for other points of view, if necessary (and we'll discuss that in a minute), you should go through your story and make sure that you are writing from your hero's point of view as much as possible.

Types of Point of View

There are a number of different points of view (POV), including the following:

- **FIRST-PERSON POV:** I thought about what it would do to my mother, but then I grabbed the gun and fired anyway. *The most intimate point of view.*
- **SECOND-PERSON POV:** You thought about what it might do to your mother, but you grabbed the gun and fired anyway. *A weird and self-conscious point of view, as you can see (apart from in how-to books). Use second person very sparingly in fiction and memoirs—if ever.*

- **THIRD-PERSON LIMITED POV:** He thought about what it would do to his mother, but then he grabbed the gun and fired anyway. *This is the preferred POV for many writers—and many genres—thanks to its versatility.*
- **OMNISCIENT POV:** He thought about what it would do to his mother, but then he grabbed the gun and fired anyway. What he didn't know was that his mother would never know, because she had already gone to Florida. *This is the author playing God—a concept considered old-fashioned by many.*
- **OBJECTIVE/DRAMATIC POV:** He grabbed the gun and fired. *The objective point of view is the point of view of the camera, which is the POV of film, television, and the theater. The audience sees what the camera sees (or what's on the stage). It's not a common choice for the novelist or memoirist, as it deprives the writer of describing the inner lives of her characters.*

As you review your second draft, you may realize you have used more than just your heroine's POV. If you're writing a crime novel, you may have scenes from your villain's point of view and maybe the victim's point of view as well. Or perhaps you're writing a love story and have alternated his and her points of view from chapter to chapter. Just remember that whenever you change your POV character, you are asking readers to shift gears, and most of the time they won't like it. They have a favorite character—your hero—and want to spend most of their time with him. That said, you can use multiple points of view, if you do it elegantly. Several authors do it elegantly: George R.R. Martin, Julia Spencer-Fleming, and Louise Penny, to name but a few.

WHEN YOUR PROTAGONIST SHOULDN'T TELL THE STORY

In some stories, the protagonist may be ill suited for the role of narrator. Take Sherlock Holmes, for example. Sir Arthur Conan Doyle tells his stories from Dr. Watson's point of view rather than his hero's. Sherlock, brilliant though he may be, is too annoying and arrogant to tell the stories in his own voice;

writing with quiet hands

he'd drive readers crazy. Dr. Watson, his friend and admirer, is perfect; readers can identify with the good doctor as he relates the stories of his cerebral if eccentric pal Sherlock. What's more, the mystery surrounding Holmes and the way his exceptional mind works remain intact.

In F. Scott Fitzgerald's *The Great Gatsby*, Nick Carraway is the everyman who narrates the story, and, like Dr. Watson to Sherlock Holmes, is a true friend to hero and man of mystery Jay Gatsby.

POV Rules to Live By

Point of view is a tricky—and touchy—subject. First of all, it's often hard to figure out—and many writers get it wrong. Mistakes in point of view are red flags to editors, who may assume before they read any further that the writer is an amateur—and stop reading altogether. Before you get all indignant on me, let me say that I've heard more than one editor complain about this publicly at conferences (and far more say the same thing behind closed doors).

I've lost too many sales to POV issues writers have refused to address. In fact, I've found that editors are *so* sensitive to POV problems that now I won't work with any writers who refuse to fix the POV—even if a writer has a great story with great characters. That said, writers who have mastered their craft have earned the right to break the rules. But you need to learn those rules first.

Here are some rules to keep in mind, rules that you break at your peril, depending upon your level of craft:

- **STICK TO FIRST-PERSON OR THIRD-PERSON LIMITED POINT OF VIEW.** As we've seen, these are the preferred points of view for contemporary fiction. With good reason.
- **IF YOU ARE USING FIRST PERSON, STICK TO ONE POV PER BOOK.** I know, I know, Gillian Flynn used multiple first-person points of view in *Gone Girl*, but this is the exception to the rule. Gillian Flynn has mastered her craft—and this was not her first successful book. Debut authors can seriously sabotage their

chances of selling their work when they use multiple first-person points of view. Editors hate this approach because it's difficult for the reader to keep track of which "I" is speaking.

- **DON'T JUMP FROM HEAD TO HEAD.** Leaping from one character's head to another willy-nilly drives editors crazy. Just don't do it.
- **STICK TO ONE POV PER SCENE.** Period. I know, I know, you see writers break this rule all the time, even in today's bestsellers, but often those writers are British, European, and/or originally published abroad (as opposed to in the United States) or were published many years ago.
- **NO MORE THAN SIX POVS PER BOOK.** Every time you switch points of view, the reader has to shift gears. The fewer POV characters you have, the better, especially if you're a debut author. A far bigger agent than I tells her big-name clients that she can't sell anything with more than six POVs—and she refuses to even try. I believe her.
- **DON'T USE OMNISCIENT POINT OF VIEW.** You might be thinking, *But I see omniscient point of view all the time in science fiction, fantasy, British mysteries, European fiction, nineteenth-century novels. ...* And you'd be right. But if you want to publish in the United States, then you need to sell American editors—and American editors tend to see omniscient point of view as old-fashioned.

One more rule (I know, I know): The writers you love may break these POV rules all the time. But I'll say it once more: It takes great craftsmanship to break them—and you do so at your peril. I can tell you lots of POV horror stories, but I'll settle for two.

The first involves screenwriters turned novelists. I have several screenwriting clients, and when they write their first novels, they often have a problem with point of view. They tend to use the objective/camera point of view instead of third person or first person—and they have to go through and fix the point of view before I can shop their work.

Other clients, in the wake of the megahit *Gone Girl,* have written stories using multiple first-person points of view. This is tough to pull off, and I usually ask writers to change this. At my request, one of my clients did a second draft in which she switched from multiple first-person POV to multiple third-person limited POV—and I got her a multi-book deal. Another client had also written a story with six first-person points of view. In her second draft, she whittled the number of POVs to three and switched them to third person. I got her a multi-book deal as well.

Who you choose to tell your story is a momentous decision—and one that will absolutely affect your ability to sell your work. So make sure that a point-of-view review is part of your second-draft deep dive.

What Happens in Your Story?

"I better make the plot good. I wanted to make it grip people on the first page and have a big turning point in the middle, as there is, and construct the whole thing like a roller-coaster ride." —MARK HADDON

You know who's telling your story. Now it's time to look at what's happening. Go through your first draft, marking up the text in different-colored markers for the following three basic elements:

1. **CONFLICT.** Conflict is the lifeblood of drama. Just as you learned in high school English class, conflict happens whenever your hero is at odds with another person (man vs. man), technology (man vs. machine), society (man vs. society), Mother Nature (man vs. nature), God (man vs. fates/gods), the supernatural (man vs. the paranormal), or even himself (man vs. himself). When your hero-

ine is fighting with her mother or hacking into the CIA database or quitting her job or exposing a political conspiracy or trying to survive a nor'easter or yelling at God or confronting a werewolf or conquering her fear of spiders—this is conflict. Without it, nothing happens. Mark these sections with a green marker.

2. **DESCRIPTION.** These are the lines, paragraphs, and/or sections in which you describe your setting, expound on theme, detail the backstory, etc. Mark them in pink.

3. **INNER LIFE.** These are the parts in which you record your character's thoughts and feelings and ruminations and navel-gazing. Mark them in yellow—and underline the sections in which your character is alone as well.

I know that you're tempted to skip this exercise. But don't. Once you finish marking up your hard copy or highlighting your file, you only have to flip or scroll through it to get a sense of the balance of these elements.

- **THE PERFECT BALANCE:** all green, with yellow and pink woven through the conflict, creating a tapestry of action
- **A GOOD BALANCE:** 75 percent green, 15 percent yellow, 10 percent pink, or thereabouts
- **A BAD BALANCE:** less than 50 percent green

Now that you know how much conflict you have in your first draft, you can amp it up in the second draft. Aim for that perfect balance.

NO MORE CHUNKS

Many beginning writers tend to write in chunks: Here's a chunk that's mostly description, followed by a chunk that's all backstory, then a chunk that's all dialogue, etc.—creating a patchwork quilt of elements that do not a seamless narrative make. If you've got a quilt on your hands, think instead of a tapestry. Each scene needs to be a tapestry of character, dialogue, action, backstory, inner monologue, and setting—all the elements woven together seamlessly.

The opening line of Harlan Coben's bestseller *Promise Me* is a masterpiece of tapestry:

> The missing girl [**character, description, backstory**]—there had been unceasing news reports, always flashing to that achingly ordinary school portrait of the vanished teen, you know the one, with the rainbow-swirl background, the girl's hair too straight, her smile too self-conscious, then a quick cut to the worried parents on the front lawn, microphones surrounding them, Mom silently tearful, Dad reading a statement with quivering lip [**backstory, character, setting, description, inner monologue**]—that girl, that *missing* girl, had just walked past Edna Skylar [**action, character**].

The weaving of all those elements—in one line, the opening line, no less—that's tapestry.

"I cut everything that stands in the way of the narrative thrust; anything that lapses beneath a certain state of tension. Because this seems to me the essence of the novel—the exact harmony between subject matter (symbolisms, intellectual, and stylistic aims) and narrative force (simple old readability). ... Narrative is a sort of magnetism." —JOHN FOWLES

Who Makes It Happen?

"The main question in drama, the way I was taught, is always, 'What does the protagonist want?' That's what drama is. It comes down to that. It's not about theme, it's not about ideas, it's not about setting, but what the protagonist wants." —DAVID MAMET

Another critical question to ask yourself as you analyze your first draft and take that deep dive into your second draft is this: Does the protagonist drive the action? Think of your story as a movie, one that every A-list actor in Hollywood is hot, hot, hot for. Why? Because it's such a great role. For an actor, that means he's the star, he's the one the movie is all about. From the moment he steps on the stage, he's got all the best lines, the best scenes, the best dramatic arc. He gets the girl, he takes the castle, he saves the world.

He may have help—friends and associates—but when the bomb is about to go off, he defuses it. Personally.

I can't tell you how many otherwise perfectly good storytellers fail to make their protagonists drive the action of their stories, from beginning to end. It's one of the most-common complaints I hear from editors—and one of the most-common plot mistakes I ask authors to fix before I send out their work. Even in crime fiction—where you'd think that common sense alone would dictate that the sleuth, amateur or professional, would solve the case and play a proactive role in the identification and apprehension of the murderer—many writers give away the best scenes to secondary characters.

So in your second draft, make sure that your likable protagonist is driving the action. Make the role one that Hollywood's A-list will be lining up to play.

You Really, Really Like Me

The other side of this coin is likability. The actors who get the best leading roles are the ones audiences like, the ones they'll pay good money to see on the screen—the Brad Pitts, George Clooneys, Tom Hanks, Jennifer Lawrences, Reese Witherspoons, and Judy Denches of the world. Even when they play truly flawed characters, audiences like them. So your protagonist needs to be likable. This means creating a character who is worth hanging out with, because he or she is funny or smart or resourceful or just plain nice.

"I write a ridiculous number of drafts. The characters change and grow through the drafting, and my

understanding of them deepens. Creating characters in a novel is like shooting at clay pigeons and
missing, and then missing more productively as the
narrative continues." —ROBERT BOSWELL

HOW TO HIRE A DEVELOPMENTAL EDITOR

A developmental edit is a "big picture" edit. A developmental editor reads your manuscript and provides commentary about your story, which typically addresses your story's premise, plot, characters, dialogue, action, conflict, language, readability, commercial potential, readiness for market, and so on. The edit usually points out your strengths, areas that need work, and recommended next steps. It is not a line edit, although some editors may include that for another fee. But don't take them up on that—you want to wait until you've done at least your second draft before you bother with a line edit. Remember: There's no point in icing a half-baked cake.

Good developmental editors are hard to find. For best results, get recommendations from a successful writer you respect, an acquisitions editor or agent, or your genre association.

COMING UP FOR AIR

Okay, you dove into your second draft and made it the best it can be. Your story rocks with conflict—and your protagonist rocks that conflict. You're ready to polish, polish, polish—until your story shines so bright that you'll need to wear shades.

HANDS ON

Cast your protagonist and make a list of all the reasons the actor you have in mind would agree to play the part. *Hint:* It should be a rather long list.

CHAPTER TWELVE

revision as ritual

"On the last drafts, I focus on the words themselves, including the rub of vowels and consonants, stressed and unstressed syllables. Yet even at this stage I'm often surprised. A different ending or a new character shows up and I'm back to where I began, letting the story happen, just trying to stay out of the way." —RON RASH

If writing a story is like building a piece of fine furniture—and let's say that it is—then congratulations. You've sawed the wood, carved the flourishes, assembled the pieces, glued them in place, stained and sealed the whole thing. Now it's time to wax. This is the polishing part of the process—and how you approach the polish determines how beautiful the final product will be. It may also determine whether you sell it.

The more you polish, the greater the shine. Publishers are as attracted to shiny objects as everyone else is. So make sure that your story is as well polished as it is compelling. This is where professionalism comes in. The willingness to comb through these final drafts with a sharp eye and a red pen is what separates the pros from the amateurs.

Being perceived as a professional is as important in publishing as it is in any other field. Perhaps more so, since too many writers see their calling as "artistes" as license to forgo the usual hallmarks of professionalism. Present company excepted, of course.

"I have to rewrite a lot. I couldn't tell you how many drafts I write, but I know I've done at least twenty rewrites on each book." —KIMBERLY WILLIS HOLT

HARNESSING YOUR INNER CRITIC

The editor in you, whom you've kept at bay while you wrote your first and second drafts, is now allowed to come out and play. Your inner editor is that smart kid from sixth grade, the precocious girl who always raised her hand for every question, the vigilant boy your teacher always put in charge of the classroom when she left the room. If this smart kid was you, then you probably count a spelling bee championship among your grammar school laurels—and you're all set. Just pretend you're grading someone else's homework, and set to work. Don't worry, I'll provide precise instructions.

If, on the other hand, you were the kid who was launching spitballs at the teacher, spent most of your time in school with your desk facing the wall, and conned your mother into writing all of your book reports while you played video games, then you might have trouble locating your inner editor. Or you may find that your inner editor is as indifferent to spelling, grammar, continuity, and the nuances of elegant sentence construction as you were when you were a kid. It's up to you to learn to pay attention and develop an eye for writerly detail.

Either way, you need some training in the art of editing. Sure, you can always hire a good line editor and/or copy editor. (You can also take a class in copyediting at your local community college or sign up for an online class—it will be money well spent.) But you should still do the best you can to edit your work yourself before you pay for help. Developmental editing is a trickier proposition than line editing, but there's no shame in hiring either or both (see the sidebar in chapter eleven). That said, it would behoove you to learn to copyedit your own work. Not doing so is like showing up for work unwashed and unkempt in shorts and flip-flops. It's simply unprofessional.

My first editor, the inestimable Tom Owens, taught me to edit my own work when I landed my first job as a reporter for a now-defunct monthly business magazine in the late 1980s. This was before the widespread adoption of PC workstations; we wrote our stories on IBM Selectric typewriters and turned our pages in to Tom, which he then returned to us marked up in red pen. We typed up the stories again, incorporating his changes, and then saved the clean copies. Once a month, during the production cycle, we collected our pages, took them into the computer room, and typed the stories into the mainframe.

This was actually far more efficient than it sounds, not so much in terms of all that typing—I was the worst typist ever, and when word processors came along shortly thereafter it made my working life exponentially easier—but in terms of learning to edit my own work. Tom marked up my pages, and I had to make those changes and type the pages all over again. Over time, I began to anticipate his remarks and to edit my stories as I wrote before I turned them in to Tom—creating a sort of editing muscle memory for prose. This saved me a lot of typing. Most important, it taught me to produce clean, clear, tightly written copy.

Within a few years, I was the editor, in charge of teaching reporters as green as I had been how to produce clean, clear, tightly written copy. We had computers by then—laptops even!—and many editors switched to editing their reporters' work electronically on the spot and sending it right along to production—rather than giving it back to the writers to incorporate their changes. It was faster, perhaps, but inefficient in terms of teaching reporters to edit themselves. I stuck to Tom's technique, editing my reporters' stories on hard copy in red pen and handing them back to the reporters to input the changes, just as Tom had done for me. They learned the art of self-editing, just as I had done.

When I traded journalism for book publishing, I was faced with the opposite problem: I had to train editors to write jacket copy (that is, the sales copy that appears on the flaps and back covers of books).

These young editors all made their living editing book-length manu-scripts directly on the computer; they were horrified at the thought of my marking up their copy in red pen on *paper*. I know they wondered why I didn't edit the pages using change tracking so they could see what I'd done and accept the changes. But they could do that with just a click on the keyboard. Better they should have to make the changes themselves to learn how to think like a writer.

Because that's what writing is—it's thinking on paper. Editing is correcting *sloppy* thinking on paper.

And now, as promised, those instructions for polishing your work.

"The beautiful part of writing is that you don't have to get it right the first time, unlike, say, a brain surgeon. You can always do it better, find the exact word, the apt phrase, the leaping simile." —ROBERT CORMIER

A QUESTION OF CRAFT

How clean is your copy? How good is your eye when it comes to catching spelling mistakes, grammatical errors, typos, re-dundancies, inconsistencies, awkward sentences, and so on?

HOW TO HIRE A LINE EDITOR OR COPY EDITOR

First, let's define our terms. *Line edit* and *copy edit* are not interchangeable terms. Copyediting addresses spelling, grammar, redundancies, repetitions, inconsistencies, and fact-checking. Line editing is all this and more, the more being reworking and even rewriting awkward sentences to address flow, clarity, etc. Most copy editors and line editors do both, and the lines blur depending on the editor and the manuscript. A heavy copy edit and a light line edit are about the same thing.

You can hire either a line editor or a copy editor to edit your entire manuscript. Or you can ask the editor to do fifty or a hundred pages, editing on hard copy so you can see what they do—and then input the changes yourself. This way, you'll learn how to do it as well. Tom would be proud.

WHEN IN DOUBT, DELETE

"I like to edit my sentences as I write them. I rearrange a sentence many times before moving on to the next one. For me, that editing process feels like a form of play, like a puzzle that needs solving, and it's one of the most satisfying parts of writing."
—KAREN THOMPSON

This is the mantra editors live by: When in doubt, delete. You may have heard the writer's version of this, which is: Murder your darlings. Generally speaking, this means that whenever you read a line you feel particularly proud of, you should lose it. Odds are you're just showing off—and to paraphrase Elmore Leonard, if it sounds like writing, you should rewrite it.

Or just hit the delete key.

As you comb through your manuscript, every time you think, *I'm not sure that works*, you'll be tempted to second guess yourself and think, *Oh, it's fine*. Think again. It's not fine. Fix it—or lose it.

The easiest way to recognize overwriting when you hear it is to read your work out loud. Yeah, you heard me right. Print out your story on hard copy, and read it out loud. Every word. Mark every passage over which you stumble in yellow marker. When you're finished, go back through and fix or lose those passages. Read it out loud again.

writing with quiet hands

"Vigorous writing is concise. A sentence should contain no unnecessary words, a paragraph no unnecessary sentences, for the same reason that a drawing should have no unnecessary lines and a machine no unnecessary parts." —WILLIAM STRUNK JR.

Cut Your Story Down to Size

Is your manuscript *way* too long? Then reading it out loud and trimming here and there won't cut it. More drastic action is needed.

Many of the queries I receive begin, "In my 200,000-word novel ..." I stop right there. As I tell all my clients, I can't sell anything by a first-time writer over 120,000 words. And I won't even try to sell a thriller over 90,000 words. (Word count requirements vary according to category; do your homework and find out what the preferred word count is for your genre these days.)

"Help me cut it," they say, knowing that I spent some fifteen years as an editor before becoming an agent. But I won't do it. Once it's cut down to size, I can help refine it. But they need to do the cutting themselves.

And so do you. Only you know your story well enough to determine its basic shape. That said, I have created guidelines that will help you make those big cuts you need to make.

Let's say that you have a manuscript that weighs in at 180,000 words. Start by answering the questions only you can answer:

- **DO YOU HAVE TWO BOOKS?** If you're writing a series or a trilogy, this might be the case. If your current manuscript is at nearly 180,000 words, you could still carve it into two 90,000-word books. This would mean that you have a storyline that could accommodate *two* structures, as follows, with each book coming in at 360 pages (250 words per page):

    ACT ONE: 90 pages (22,500 words)
    ACT TWO: 180 pages (45,000 words)
    ACT THREE: 90 pages (22,500 words)

- **OR DO YOU HAVE ONE BOOK THAT IS SIMPLY TOO LONG?** In which case you need to cut it down to 120,000 words, which is 480 pages (250 words per page):

    ACT ONE: 120 pages (30,000 words)
    ACT TWO: 240 pages (60,000 words)
    ACT THREE: 120 pages (30,000 words)

Answer these questions by writing out the basic storyline in your plot points only (for a refresher on plot points, see chapter six): *Inciting Incident, Plot Point 1, Midpoint, Plot Point 2, Denouement.* Breaking it down into these basic chunks should help you figure out if you have one book or two. You can then break it down into acts.

Once you have the acts and accompanying plot points, you can cut your story to the word counts I've outlined above. This should be easy, because anything that doesn't get you from plot point to plot point *must go.*

DRILL IT DOWN

Get a writer friend to exchange ten pages of manuscript with you. Now edit each other's work on hard copy with a red pen. Share these edits, and explain why you marked up what you marked up. Is your work better? Is theirs? What did you learn about your ability to edit?

"My basic rule for action scenes is that, as a reader, I want to see it. I want to feel it. So as a writer, if the words aren't helping me see and feel very clearly what's happening, then I need to choose different words. ... Each word should have the same impact as a landed punch." —ADAM STERNBERGH

PRINCIPLED POLISHING

You can use certain polishing principles to buff your story to a perfect gloss. Here are some steps for that final review:

- **CHECK YOUR CHARACTERS' NAMES.** It's better if you stick with character names that are: (1) easy to read, pronounce, and spell (so the reader doesn't stumble over them every time as she reads); (2) not too similar to other characters' names in your story (so the reader doesn't stop reading to figure out who's who all the time); and (3) are in keeping with the gender, background, and even temperament of the character.
- **DON'T WRITE IN DIALECT.** Ever. It drives editors crazy. Use word choice, sentence structure, etc., to indicate dialect.
- **TONE DOWN THE HYPERBOLE.** The more dramatic the story, the more you need to tell it straight. There's no reason to use hyperbolic language; the action is dramatic enough. You need to tone down the hyperbole—otherwise you fall into melodrama, undermine your authority as a storyteller, and lose the true impact of your story.
- **USE AMERICAN ENGLISH.** If you are submitting to an American publisher, agent, or editor, you need to use American grammar, spelling, and punctuation.
- **RUN A READING LEVEL ON YOUR PROSE.** This is one of the best ways to make sure that your prose is engaging and easy to read. If you are writing in Microsoft Word (which you should be, as that's the standard for submission), you'll find the reading level under

the Review tab in the Spelling and Grammar tool. (*Note:* Make sure that you've checked the "show readability statistics" box in the options under Spelling and Grammar.) Then when you run the Spelling and Grammar tool, the Flesch-Kincaid reading level will show up under readability statistics. This level refers to the grade level of reading proficiency needed to comprehend a given work. The average newspaper in the United States is written at a sixth-grade reading level, so if yours comes in at anything much above that, you need to simplify your prose. Aim for a reading level between sixth and eighth grade.

- **WATCH YOUR DIALOGUE TAGS.** Don't use dialogue tags like *queried, proclaimed, pondered,* etc. That drives editors crazy. Stick to *said.* Or use action instead. Craig Johnson, best-selling author of the Longmire series, never uses any dialogue tags. He uses action only.

> "Stop!" he proclaimed. (bad)
>
> "Stop!" he said. (better)
>
> "Stop!" He pointed his gun straight at me. (best)

- **LOSE THE CLICHÉS.** Common turns of phrase—hot as hell, cold as ice, soft as butter—clutter up your prose and diminish your style.
- **SWAP OUT WEAK VERBS FOR STRONG VERBS.** Weak verbs include all forms of "to be" as well as the tired verbs we use all the time. Why say *talk* when you can say *whisper, communicate, inform, debate, sing, pronounce, murmur, mutter, mumble, express, clarify, vocalize, verbalize, chat, chatter, gab, yak, discuss, articulate, converse, enunciate, tell, gossip,* or *confess?*
- **LOSE THE ADVERBS.** If you've used strong verbs, you don't need adverbs. Seriously.
- **STIR UP THE READER'S SENSES.** Arm the language of your story with all of the senses. As you go through your manuscript, make

sure that the reader can see, hear, touch, smell, and taste the world in which your story takes place.

"Good writing is supposed to evoke sensation in the reader—not the fact that it is raining, but the feeling of being rained upon." —E.L. DOCTOROW

HANDS ON

Hemingway started every morning's work by reading his story from the beginning, editing as he went. Even when the story grew very long, he would read the last two or three chapters before beginning to write—and once a week, he'd read it from the beginning again. This was how he made it, in his words, "all of one piece." Adopt this practice, so you, too, can stay in your story through draft after draft.

"You write to communicate to the hearts and minds of others what's burning inside you. And we edit to let the fire show though the smoke."
—ARTHUR POLOTNIK

PART THREE

writer meets world

writ·er

noun \'rī-tər\

: someone whose work is to write books, poems, stories, etc.

Old English *writere* "one who can write, clerk; one who produces books or literary compositions," agent noun from *writan*; meaning "sign-painter" is from 1837.

world

noun \'wər(-ə)ld\

the world : the earth and all the people and things on it

: a part of the world and the people and things that exist there

: human society

Old English *woruld*, *worold* "human existence, the affairs of life," also "a long period of time," also "the human race, mankind, humanity," a word peculiar to Germanic languages (cognates: Old Saxon *werold*, Old Frisian *warld*, Dutch *wereld*, Old Norse *verold*, Old High German *weralt*, German *Welt*), with a literal sense of "age of man," from Proto-Germanic *wer* "man" (Old English *wer*, still in werewolf) and *ald* "age"

CHAPTER THIRTEEN

devices and desire

"... As far as productivity goes in writing, I just find a quiet life is much the best kind to write out of. It is true that you need to kind of know what makes the world go around so entire quietness isn't to be desired either, but by and large regular habits and making a firm alliance with a few people seems to me to be a nice way for this particular set of genes and muscles to go through our vale of tears." —JOHN UPDIKE

Writing with quiet hands means writing from a calm and centered, energized and engaged place. That said, maintaining that kind of grace and grit during the creative process can be a challenge. Approaching writing as a craft can help you avoid the dubious devices some writers use to face the blank page.

Or, as Hunter S. Thompson put it: "I hate to advocate drugs, alcohol, violence, or insanity to anyone, but they've always worked for me." Not really, since he blew his brains out, just like his idol, Ernest Hemingway, did. Both were great writers who died too soon.

These are extreme examples, to be sure, but the writing life does present a number of greater and lesser challenges that can interfere with the happy production of good work. Better to adopt a role model like John Updike, whose craftsman-like approach to his work resulted in an astounding body of work—novels, short stories, poems, essays, and criticism described by the *New York Times* as "so vast, protean, and lyrical as to place him in the first rank of American authors."

Updike dedicated his mornings and early afternoons to writing in his study on the second floor of his home in Beverly Farms, Massachusetts, setting a quota of at least three pages a day. He was a man of work habits, who, when asked what advice he would give writers, invariably spoke of work habits and quotas. Joyce Carol Oates, another prolific author of the first order, writes every day, "almost all day long with interruptions" in her study upstairs (as Updike did) in her home not far from Princeton. Both have been accused of writing too much, but neither Updike nor Oates, longtime friends, put much stock in the idea that their productivity was exceptional in any way. Updike called himself and his pal Oates "blue-collar writers" who approached the business of writing seriously and applied their writing energies in an orderly way—as opposed to devoting those energies to "the pursuit of the good life and happiness and drugs and drink and celebrity." Writers with good work habits can write "an alarming amount" over the course of a lifetime.

You, too, can write an alarming amount over the course of your lifetime, if you form good work habits and avoid the distractions that may lie in wait along the writer's path.

"I've had very little experience in my life. In fact, I try to avoid experience if I can. Most experience is bad."
—E.L. DOCTOROW

A QUESTION OF CRAFT

Do you lead an organized life? Are you a writer of good work habits? How do your work habits—good or bad—help or hinder your productivity? What might you do to enhance your productivity?

KEEPING THE DRAMA ON THE PAGE

"Writing is a form of therapy; sometimes I wonder how all those who do not write, compose, or paint can manage to escape the madness, melancholia, the panic and fear which is inherent in a human situation." —GRAHAM GREENE

My talented client Richard writes very dark noir, so dark that many editors found his work too relentlessly bleak to publish. We're talking Cormac McCarthy dark here. But he's a wonderful writer, and I knew we'd find the right editor for him eventually. And we did.

When the editor from a Big Five publishing house called me to make an offer on Richard's novel, I told him that I'd have to get back to him, but that it might take me awhile, as I knew that he was on vacation at Disney World with his family.

"Disney World?" The editor laughed. "I find it hard to believe that the guy who wrote this story, of all stories, is at The Happiest Place on Earth. That's the last place I'd expect to find him."

Richard may write about mean streets and psychopaths, evil deeds and bad ends, but in real life he's a family man working on his master of fine arts. His work may be the stuff of nightmares, but his writing life is organized, ordinary, and productive. Richard is a craftsman of the first order—and he's got five Pushcart Prize nominations and a multi-book deal to prove it.

The trick is to keep the drama on the page. Be a blue-collar writer: Sit down every day and write. When real life threatens to overwhelm your writing life, fight back. If you've formed good work habits, you'll be better prepared to ride out the days of drama that we all inevitably face—and write right through them.

"First forget inspiration. Habit is more dependable. Habit will sustain you whether you're inspired or not. Habit will help you finish and polish your stories. Inspiration won't. Habit is persistence in practice." —Octavia E. Butler

BLOCK(ED) HEAD

"Writer's block is my unconscious mind telling me that something I've just written is either unbelievable or unimportant to me, and I solve it by going back and reinventing some part of what I've already written so that when I write it again, it is believable and interesting to me. Then I can go on." —Orson Scott Card

Some writers claim that there is no such thing as writer's block. That real writers write, no matter what. Tell that to best-selling author and humorist Fran Lebowitz, who suffered from what she called "writer's blockade" for decades.

She's not alone. I know writers who have agonized over an inability to write—for weeks, months, years, and more. Sometimes, despite all best efforts, writer's block happens. I know, because it happened to me. I'd been a professional writer and editor for ten years—and then I stopped writing my own work. I still wrote and edited at work—copywriting, ghostwriting, editing, and rewriting other people's projects—but I simply stopped working on my own projects.

I could no longer face the page.

At the time, my life was all about drama—one familial and financial disaster after another—and I lost myself in the chaos. I couldn't face the truth of my life, and so I couldn't face the page. Because writing is about telling the truth, one way or another. After nearly ten years of silence, I found my voice again, and I started writing again. By this time I'd made big changes in my life—got a divorce, moved across the country, bought a house—and my life was relatively drama-free. More important, I'd found myself again—and what I found was a writer ready to tell the truth once more.

Pour your nightmares, sorrows, and obsessions into your work. Too much drama in your real life can keep you from writing your best work, or from writing for a lifetime, or from writing altogether. Drama in real life is ultimately exhausting and can exhaust your talent and your drive, not to mention your body, mind, and soul. Burnout, for many writers, equals writer's block. And for a writer, writer's block is a kind of death.

Other Reasons You May Be Blocked

"I pretty much drink a cup of coffee, write in my journal for a while, and then sit at a computer in my office and torture the keys. My one saving grace as a writer is that, if I'm having trouble with the novel I'm writing, I write something else, a poem or a short story. I try to avoid writer's block by always writing something." —JESS WALTER

If your life is relatively drama-free, then there may be other factors affecting your ability to get your work done. Most of these have to do with fear, perfectionism, and unpreparedness. Here are some strategies to help you deal with these issues:

WORK ON MORE THAN ONE PROJECT AT A TIME. Isaac Asimov worked on up to a dozen or more projects at a time. He placed tables with typewriters around the perimeter of his study, one typewriter for each project. He'd sit down every morning at the first typewriter, work on that project until he got stuck, and then move on to the next typewriter—and the next project. He wrote or edited more than five hundred books in his lifetime, from classic science fiction novels like *I, Robot* to works on Shakespeare, science, and history.

Most of us couldn't keep all those projects in our heads at one time—and I, for one, wouldn't even want to try. But many writers have at least two projects in progress at any given time, mixing up fiction and nonfiction, book-length works and shorter pieces.

DO MORE RESEARCH. You may need to prime your pump to keep the words flowing. If you've run out of gas, then you need to go back for more source material. To paraphrase Dr. Samuel Johnson, you may have to turn over half the library to make one book. Do more research, conduct more interviews, dig deeper into your material, and go about "poking and prying with a purpose," as Zora Neale Hurston put it. Priming your pump is often enough to kick-start your subconscious and get your juju back.

BACK-BURNER YOUR STORY FOR TWENTY-FOUR HOURS. Sometimes you just need a break from the story to let your subconscious work out whatever storytelling problem is holding you back. Tell your subconscious that you are taking this one day off and that you are not going to think about your story. Put it on the back burner—but don't leave the room. Organize your files, paint a wall red, build some bookshelves. Stay in your work space—and try not to write. By the time the paint dries, you should be ready for work.

LOWER YOUR EXPECTATIONS. Malcolm Gladwell swears by this technique—and, per usual, he's on to something. Perfectionism is the worst kind of sabotage—and can shut down your creativity with a hard stop. So give yourself permission to write badly. Very badly. Your mantra: *I'll fix it later. I'll fix it later. I'll fix it later.*

I use this one all the time, because I tend to think that every day's work is awful. But I tell myself that I'll fix it later, and I shut off my laptop when I've met my word count goal for the day. The next morning, I reread what I wrote the day before, and it's almost always better than I thought it would be. If it's not, I fix it.

DRILL IT DOWN

Add another project to your works in progress. If you're writing a novel, start writing a nonfiction article for your local newspaper or a blog for your company website. If you're writing a full-length memoir, try writing a short story in your favorite fiction genre. Divide your writing time; for instance, work on one in the morning and the other in the afternoon.

"Writer's block is only a failure of the ego."
—NORMAN MAILER

QUESTION YOUR MOTIVES

George Orwell believed that there are four things that motivate writers to write:

1. **SHEER EGOISM.** These writers write because they want to honor what they see as their talent, individualism, and/or superiority.
2. **AESTHETIC ENTHUSIASM.** These writers write because they value the beauty of the word, the puzzle of wordplay, the pattern of prose, the structure of story, and/or even the look of the typography on the page.
3. **HISTORICAL IMPULSE.** These writers write because they are driven to discover the truth and record it for posterity.
4. **POLITICAL PURPOSE.** These writers write because they have a belief, a cause, or a societal objective to put forward.

Which motivations resonate with you? One or two or even all of these factors may be driving your desire to write. Knowing

> why you write is critical to creating, maintaining, and sustaining your desire to do the work and get it out there. It can also help you avoid burnout or overcome writer's block when it threatens to derail your work. By acknowledging your motivation and fueling it, you can keep your career on track.

"Tears are words that need to be written."
—PAULO COELHO

THE MINDFUL ART OF DISTRACTION

"The only time I really feel I can get away from the physical act of writing is when I am running or walking, because then I can think about the writing from another perspective." —JOYCE CAROL OATES

One of the best things you can do to exercise your writing muscles has nothing to do with writing at all. It has to do with the rest of your body. Study after study reveals that thirty minutes of moderate physical activity three or four days a week literally grows your brain.

You may not want to hear this. But odds are that if you spend enough time writing, you're going to get what we call in the newspaper business "writer's spread." When I was editing an alternative weekly newspaper in Northern California more than twenty years ago, I took one of my junior reporters with me to a newspaper conference in Los Angeles. We were sitting in the hotel ballroom with some five hundred journalists when the twenty-five-year-old writer turned to me and said, "If I stay in this business, am I going to be fat, too?" I looked around, and sure enough, the majority of the middle-aged people in the room were noticeably overweight. This was anathema to my native Californian colleague, who'd grown up where everyone was a slim vegetarian—or trying to be.

The truth is, sitting on your butt long enough to write a body of work is going to take a toll. Even if you're slender, you may suffer from back trouble or neck pain or carpal tunnel syndrome. New studies say that "sitting is the new smoking"—that's how bad it is for you.

Not to mention that as writers we tend to be in our heads a lot—or as my mother used to tell me, "You think too much." Physical activity is the perfect antidote to all that sitting and thinking. If you do nothing else, do this: (1) get up and move around for ten minutes of every hour you spend seated and (2) take that thirty-minute walk every other day, if not every day. Do it for your body and your brain—and don't forget: As we saw in chapter two, many successful writers count their daily walk as a way to summon the muse.

The Om of Writing

"It's all about paying attention." —SUSAN SONTAG

You already know that yoga and meditation practice is a big part of my writing life; it keeps me centered and calm and helps me write with quiet hands. But yoga and meditation have physical and mental benefits as well.

Yoga keeps you flexible and can help relieve back and neck pain, arthritis, and carpal tunnel syndrome that often afflict us writers. I suffered a neck injury as a child, and it flares up whenever I sit hunched over my laptop too long (in what my yoga teacher trainer calls "computer asana"). But as long as I do my yoga practice, I remain relatively pain-free.

Deep breathing and meditation—with or without yoga—are beneficial as well. Learning to quiet the mind and pay attention to the breath can help you do the following:

- lower blood pressure, relieve depression and anxiety, reduce stress, improve mood and behavior, boost the immune system, and increase energy levels.
- improve focus, enhance creativity, increase happiness, develop intuition, gain clarity, and promote emotional stability.

Many of my most prolific clients are active people who balance their writing time with physical activity. Two are yoga teachers, and two are farmers. There's a stay-at-home mom in New Jersey and a stay-at-home dad in Chicago and a stay-at-home mom in Australia who all juggle writing with running around after their respective small children. Two are chefs running restaurants, and two are martial arts experts, and several more are law enforcement and/or military personnel who work out religiously. You may prefer gardening or golfing (skip the cart and walk) or hiking or biking or swimming. Anything that keeps your body moving and your brain chilling is good for your writing. So just do it.

Writing is not for the faint of heart. Writing well requires mental acuity, emotional courage, and physical stamina. Staying in good shape—mind, body, and spirit—is critical to doing good work.

"The imagination needs moodling—long, inefficient happy idling, dawdling, and puttering."
—BRENDA UELAND

HANDS ON

For every hour you spend writing, spend half an hour walking or practicing yoga or doing some kind of physical activity. Build this into your schedule, and see how this balance benefits your writing life.

CHAPTER FOURTEEN

good writers and good friends

"It's a cliché, but true, that writing is intensely solitary and at times really lonely. I sit in one room and talk to squirrels and blue jays all day."
—DOUGLAS COUPLAND

Every writer must make his peace with the loneliness that often accompanies the writing life. Doing good work requires solitude; even when you are sitting in a room filled with family, à la Jane Austen, you're still alone with your thoughts and your pen. You're on your own in your head—and that head can be a lonely place.

No writer walks alone. Just as we need to balance the mental exertion of writing with physical activity, we need to balance the solitude of writing with meaningful relationships with friends and family. They are the people who know and love us, despite our writerly peculiarities. We just can't expect them to understand us.

If you want to feel understood, then you need to make some writer friends. Some writers will tell you not to hang out with other writers because they can be petty and jealous and/or steal your ideas. I've never found that to be true (but you still shouldn't share your high-concept ideas with anyone you don't know well and don't trust completely).

I've always loved hanging out with writers; most of my friends, old and new, are writers. When I moved to the Northeast after many years in California, I missed my writer friends. I was working as an acquisitions editor for a publisher in northern Massachusetts, surrounded by publishing people all day, but publishing people are not necessarily writing people. I still missed hanging out with writers. My Florida friend, Edgar-winner Trish MacGregor, advised me to get active in Mystery Writers of America. I joined the New England chapter, and I now count many of my dearest friends (and clients) among its members.

We live in a world of writers and nonwriters, friends and family, colleagues and acquaintances, cohorts and rivals. We must learn to interact with these people in a way that secures our solitude, nourishes our work, and gives us the love and support we need as writers and as individuals. We all want to be good friends and colleagues, spouses and parents—without sacrificing our writing. This can prove a juggling act—and requires commitment, compromise, and even a little extortion.

A QUESTION OF CRAFT

How supportive of your writing are your friends and family? How does that support—or sabotage—manifest itself? How do you handle it?

"What is hell to a writer? Hell is being too busy to find the time to write or being unable to find the inspiration. Hell is suddenly finding the words but being away from your notebook or typewriter. Hell is when the verses slip away through your fingers and they never return again." —R.M. ENGELHARDT

SABOTAGE

"Be ruthless about protecting writing days, i.e., do not cave in to endless requests to have 'essential' and 'long overdue' meetings on those days. The funny thing is that, although writing has been my actual job for several years now, I still seem to have to fight for time in which to do it. Some people do not seem to grasp that I still have to sit down in peace and write the books, apparently believing that they pop up like mushrooms without my connivance. I must therefore guard the time allotted to writing as a Hungarian Horntail guards its firstborn egg." —J.K. ROWLING

Okay, if J.K. Rowling—arguably the most successful writer alive today—has to fight for time to write, what are the rest of us supposed to do? We have jobs and kids and elderly parents and mortgages and taxes and tuition and meals to cook and dogs to walk and lawns to mow and God knows what else, mostly without the benefit of a billion-dollar net worth. All these responsibilities—and the people to whom we're responsible—can make it difficult to get our writing done.

When I was a very young stay-at-home mom with two small children and a mostly absent (first) husband, I spotted an ad in the local paper announcing a meeting about the formation of a women's writing group. I got a sitter and went to that meeting. We formed a group, and eventually we started meeting at my house, since I was the only one with little kids and this spared me the expense of a babysitter. My husband, Mark, who was rarely home apart from the weekends, started coming home on the writing-group nights. I'd feed the family, put the kids to bed, and then get ready for the meeting. He'd more or less pester me the entire time. He'd disappear into our bedroom and then yell for me as soon as he heard my writer friends arrive. He'd say we were too noisy and that he couldn't sleep. He'd ask for water. When I ignored him, the phone would ring (this is in the time before answering machines) and I'd pick it up, only to be told by my husband's friend Rick that Mark wanted me to be quiet, that I was laughing too loudly again.

This was active sabotage, and it continued in one form or another until we divorced (no surprise there). By the time we separated, I'd learned my lesson. Writing was important to me, and I wouldn't let anyone take my writing time—or my writers' group—away from me.

I've heard lots of horror stories about sabotage over the years:

- Back in the floppy-disk days of computers, I worked with a journalist whose girlfriend shredded the floppy disk with all of his work on it in a fit of pique. "You need a new girlfriend," I told him. And I meant it.

- Another writer friend gave her father a copy of her newly published book—and he gave it back to her with red marks on the pages where he'd found typos. (When this happens to you, and it invariably will, just say what I always do: "That's why God made reprint corrections.")

- My girlfriend wrote a novel, and when she gave it to her mother to read, her mom—who mistakenly believed that one of the characters was modeled on her—refused to speak to her for a year.

- One of my clients recently reported that, even though she has a nanny, she goes to Starbucks to work because her kids simply won't leave her alone long enough for her to finish her writing.

- One of my writer friends gave his novel to his professor to read— and the prof told him it was terrible and that he should put it in a drawer and forget about it. A couple of years later, the professor published that novel under his own name. My friend never would have known if one of the guys in his writers' group hadn't bought the book and remembered it.

- Even the rich and famous are not immune. Ernest Hemingway's first wife left the only copy of his work on a train, never to be seen again. He later said that in retrospect, this loss proved a good thing, as it forced him to rewrite. But still.

You may suffer similar sabotage at the hands of your friends, family, and colleagues. They may mean well—or not. The motivation may vary, too—they envy your talent, they're possessive of your time, they worry you'll use them as material, they're simply negative people—but the effect is the same. They can silence you if you let them.

Ultimately it's up to each of us, as artists, to make sure that we (1) surround ourselves with people who respect our desire to write, (2) honor our writing selves, and (3) keep our promises to ourselves.

"If you show someone something you've written, you give them a sharpened stake; lie down in your coffin, and say, 'When you're ready.'" —DAVID MITCHELL

WRITE IT DOWN

Get pen and paper, and set the timer for fifteen minutes. Write about the last time someone sabotaged your writing efforts, consciously or unconsciously, subtly or blatantly. What did you do about it? If nothing, what will you do next time?

SUPPORT

"If you write fiction, you're by yourself. There are certain advantages to that in that you don't have to explain anything to anybody. But when you get in with others who share the loneliness of the whole enterprise, you're not lonely anymore." —DENIS JOHNSON

Enlisting the support of your friends, family, and fellow writers is critical to your success. And it makes your writing life so much easier. Here are some rules to live by to ensure that you're getting the encouragement and assistance you need:

good writers and good friends   195

- **OFFER TIT FOR TAT.** If your significant other resents the time you spend on your writing, then negotiate a tit-for-tat swap. For every guilt-free hour you spend writing or at writing events, your partner gets a guilt-free hour to shop or work out or spend time with pals. If you have kids, this can be particularly effective, as you can offer to watch them while your partner gets some "me" time—and vice versa.
- **TAKE A WRITING CLASS.** A class is a great place to meet other writers as well as work on your craft. There are many places where you can find great instructors and valuable instruction—from continuing-education classes at your local community college and workshops run by groups like Grub Street, Gotham, and the Algonkian New York Pitch Conferences to online seminars, classes, and boot camps run by Writer's Digest. I've taken hundreds of classes, seminars, and workshops over the years— and I've benefited from every one. Now I teach them as well—and I learn even more from my students than I did from my teachers.
- **JOIN A WRITERS' GROUP.** As I've said elsewhere in this book, a writers' group can be a wonderful incentive to write as well as an encouragement to keep writing. The trick is to find the right writers to participate. You want people who are committed to writing, will produce and share pages, and will give constructive criticism. You also want to make sure that you're not the best writer in the group. Finding a writers' group is like buying a house—you don't want the best house on the block—you want to buy "up." You don't want to be the best writer in the group; you want to learn "up" from the writers in the group who are more experienced and (hopefully) published. Keep the group small—six to eight writers, tops—and don't be afraid to ask people to leave if they prove difficult or unreliable or incapable of giving or receiving constructive criticism. Anyone who monopolizes the group or is relentlessly negative should be asked to leave. If you don't know any writers, befriend some (see the next bullet), and start your own group. If you live in a remote area, you can use Skype or Google+ to conduct your meetings with writers in various locations.

writing with quiet hands

"Remember: When people tell you something's wrong or doesn't work for them, they are almost always right. When they tell you exactly what they think is wrong and how to fix it, they are almost always wrong." —NEIL GAIMAN

- **JOIN A WRITERS' ORGANIZATION.** Every genre has its association (see the upcoming sidebar). Find yours and join. *Now.* Not only will you meet other writers, you'll be able to take advantage of the organization's many benefits, which typically include mentors; classes; information on publishers, editors, and the marketplace; PR and marketing assistance; speakers' bureaus; and more. Most organizations have online chapters as well, so if you live in a remote area, you can connect with writers all over the country, if not the world. When I first moved to Chico, California, some years ago, I was too far away to attend Mystery Writers of America meetings in San Francisco. So I looked up writers in my city in the member directory, called one, and invited her to lunch. We hit it off and invited more writers from the directory to join us in a writers' group.
- **GO TO A WRITERS CONFERENCE.** This is another great way to learn more about writing, publishing, and the marketplace. You'll have the opportunity to meet writers, agents, editors, and publishers. Not to mention these events are so much fun! There are writers conferences for every genre and sensibility, coast to coast and abroad. If you're timid, take a writer friend with you. Take advantage of everything the conference offers: Attend the banquet, go to all the sessions that time allows, and hang out in the bar (because that's where all the interesting people end up after hours). Channel your inner Oscar Wilde, and work the room!
- **ELIMINATE NEGATIVITY.** The last thing you need as a writer is people insulting you, your work, or even publishing. (As somebody once tweeted: "Give someone a book, they'll read for a day. Teach someone how to write a book, they'll experience a lifetime

of paralyzing self-doubt.") Listen only to constructive criticism and helpful information. Don't let anyone discourage you in any way. I hear people talk about the death of books all the time—but they've been having that discussion for thirty years. The book business has gone through great transition—as has all retailing—and that transition is bound to continue. People ask me why I became an agent in the middle of all this change, as if it were preordained that I would fail right along with publishing. I'll tell you what I tell them: There's plenty of opportunity during times of transition, but only if you take advantage of it. Someone's going to make it—it may as well be you.

- **FIND A MENTOR.** The best part about writers' groups and organizations and conferences is that they give you the chance to meet writers who are farther along the publishing path than you are—writers from whom you can learn and who might be willing to mentor you. You may be lucky enough to encounter some of your favorite writers and even befriend them. You'll also meet new favorites. Be nice to everyone, go to their book signings, and buy their books. Do keep in touch with everyone you can. These contacts will come in handy sooner or later—especially when it's time to find an agent, get endorsements, promote and market your work, and so on.

- **PRIME THE PUMP.** Now that you've made writer friends—you have made some writer friends by now, right?—ask one to join you on what Julia Cameron calls an "artist's date." This is anything fun that appeals to the artist in you: concerts, art exhibits, films, readings, literary events and pilgrimages ... whatever feeds your writer's soul. As I've mentioned, my writer friend Susan and I have been rewarding ourselves with artist's dates on a regular basis for years—we've been to jazz festivals and book festivals, countless movies and plays and book signings, galleries and museums, and most of the literary landmarks in the Northeast—from Emily Dickinson's house to the House of Seven Gables.

- **GIVE BACK.** Most of these communities are very supportive, and you'll want to be very supportive in return. Publishing is all about relationships, so be sure to cultivate good relationships, return favors, promote goodwill, and build up good book karma.

"... Keep on writing. Don't listen to people who tell you that very few people get published and you won't be one of them. Don't listen to your friend who says you are better than Tolkien and don't have to try any more. Keep writing, keep faith in the idea that you have unique stories to tell, and tell them."
—ROBIN HOBB

A (VERY INCOMPLETE) LIST OF WRITERS' ORGANIZATIONS

- American Society of Journalists & Authors (ASJA)
- American Society of Composers, Authors and Publishers (ASCAP)
- Association of Writers and Writing Programs (AWP)
- Authors Guild
- Dramatists Guild of America
- International Federation of Journalists (IFJ)
- International Thriller Writers (ITW)
- Investigative Reporters and Editors (IRE)
- Mystery Writers of America (MWA)
- National Association of Science Writers (NASW)
- National Writers Union (NWU)
- The Newspaper Guild (Communications Workers of America) and The Guild Reporter
- Novelists, Inc.
- PEN America
- PEN New England (PEN+NE)
- Poets & Writers (PW)
- Romance Writers of America (RWA)
- Science Fiction and Fantasy Writers of America, Inc. (SFWA)

- Sisters in Crime (SinC)
- Society for Technical Communication (STC)
- Society of American Travel Writers (SATW)
- Society of Children's Book Writers and Illustrators (SCBWI)
- Songwriters Guild of America
- Society of Professional Journalists (SPJ)
- Text and Academic Authors Association (TAA)
- Western Writers of America, Inc. (WWA)
- Writers Guild of America, West (WGAW)

DRILL IT DOWN

Join your genre writers' organization. If you already belong, go to more meetings. If you already attend all of the meetings, volunteer to help out in any way you can. The contacts—and friends—you make will serve you well.

AND THE WISDOM TO KNOW THE DIFFERENCE

"It's part of a writer's profession, as it's part of a spy's profession, to prey on the community to which he's attached, to take away information—often in secret—and to translate that into intelligence for his masters, whether it's his readership or his spy masters. And I think that both professions are perhaps rather lonely." —JOHN LE CARRÉ

Being a writer means making peace with (1) the solitude you need to do the work; (2) the connection you need to establish and maintain with the publishing community; and (3) the people you need to befriend to get the work done, build relationships with your fellow writers and potential mentors, and get your name out there.

This peacemaking begins at home. Not only with your friends and family, who may or may not understand or appreciate your commitment to the writing craft, but with your writing self. Writers come in two types: the extroverts, for whom all the solitude needed to do the work may seem like an overabundance of loneliness, and the introverts, who'd rather just stay at home and write than venture out in the world and talk to anyone about it.

To find a place in today's tough publishing environment, you need to master your craft and your marketplace. You need to secure and sit tight in the solitude you need to write and edit and polish your stories—and then you need to go out and test the waters with your fellow writers, editors, and assorted publishing professionals.

You've got the goods; now it's time to sell 'em.

"I have people in my life, of course. Some write; some don't. Some read; some don't. Some stare vacantly into space when I talk the geeky talk and walk the geeky walk, but they make killer chocolate chip pancakes and so all is forgiven." —ROB THURMAN

HANDS ON

Ask your best writer friend to join you on an artist's date. Do something fun. Schedule these outings at least twice a month—and go!

"It is not often that someone comes along who is a *true friend* and a *good writer*." —E.B. WHITE

CHAPTER FIFTEEN

agents and other oddities

"I wrote a book. It sucked. I wrote nine more books. They sucked, too. Meanwhile, I read every single thing I could find on publishing and writing, went to conferences, joined professional organizations, hooked up with fellow writers in critique groups, and didn't give up. Then I wrote one more book."
—BETH REVIS

You've written a story. You've polished and polished and polished. You've made writer friends and are part of a publishing community. You've done everything you can to prepare for the next hurdle: publishing your work.

This is where the real fun starts.

CONSORTING WITH THE FRENEMY

The good news is that there are many more publishing options for writers than there used to be. In the old days, there were two avenues: traditional publishing and vanity publishing. Very few writers published by a vanity publisher—apart from the occasional poet—

were taken seriously. The only respectable option was traditional publishing.

That was then; this is now. Self-publishing is a viable option for many writers, notably those who (1) are writing for reasons of legacy more than career and/or (2) are marketing whizzes who can sell their own books. If this describes you, then you may be happy going the self-pushing route.

But if you prefer the traditional route, then you need to find a way to get your work read by the decision makers who can publish your work. This means pitching your work to agents and editors.

DO YOU REALLY NEED AN AGENT?

Writers are always coming up to me and telling me that they don't need me. "I don't need an agent," they say. I smile sweetly and say, "Okay." I try not to laugh when they then proceed to pitch their projects to me.

Look, I love writers, and I need clients. But I receive thousands of queries a year—and I represent only a few dozen clients. Every agent is similarly bombarded by writers who want to get their work in front of the Big Five: Penguin Random House, HarperCollins, Hachette Book Group (HBG), Macmillan, and Simon and Schuster. And the easiest way to do that is through an agent. Most of the acquisitions editors who work for big houses—and many medium-size publishers as well—accept submissions only through agents. Why? Because if I get thousands of queries a year, imagine how many they get—and how many more they'd get if they accepted queries from writers directly.

It's possible to make end runs around this system. You can meet editors at writers conferences and pitch them there. You can also strike up a conversation through social media or at book signings or other publishing events. You can ask your writer friends for referrals. If one of these strategies works, and you get through to an editor who then makes you an offer,

say, "Thank you for your interest; let me talk to my agent."
Don't agree to any terms; just say thank you, hang up, and
then call the agent of your choice. Why? Because the easiest
way to get an agent is to get an offer first.

End runs aside, you should try to get an agent if you want
to go the traditional publishing route.

A QUESTION OF CRAFT

Which publishing route would you most like to take? What
are your publishing goals? What have you done in pursuit of
those goals?

PITCH, PROCESS, PERSIST

"Above all, a query letter is a sales pitch, and it is the
single most important page an unpublished writer will ever write. It's the first impression and will
either open the door or close it. It's that important,
so don't mess it up. Mine took seventeen drafts and
two weeks to write." —NICHOLAS SPARKS

Pitching is an art unto itself. It's a sales pitch, really—and you should
write one that you can use to pitch anyone, anywhere—at conferences,
in elevators, in queries. This way you can make the most of every opportunity you may have to introduce your book to agents and editors.

Write out your pitch in advance, and hone it until it sings. Let's
take a hard look at what makes a good pitch.

A Step-By-Step Elevator Pitch Breakdown

Step One: Describe your book in fifty words or less.
This description should include the following:

A TITLE: I know you've heard that titles don't matter and that publishers change them anyway—so why bother? Titles often do change, but nonetheless you need to come up with a strong title before you pitch your work. Research the titles of best-selling books in your genre to see what kinds of titles are working well. Here are some possible titling conventions to help you brainstorm one of your own:

- **OBJECTS OF DESIRE:** *The Maltese Falcon* by Dashiell Hammett; *The Secret* by Rhonda Byrne; *The Lost Symbol* by Dan Brown
- **ACTION:** *Get Shorty* by Elmore Leonard; *Eat This, Not That!* by David Zinczenko; *The Escape* by David Baldacci
- **ONE-LINERS:** *The Postman Always Rings Twice* by James M. Cain; *If You're Not First, You're Last* by Grant Cardone; *Kindness Goes Unpunished* by Craig Johnson
- **SETTING:** *Shutter Island* by Dennis Lehane; *The Pacific* by Hugh Ambrose; *South of Broad* by Pat Conroy
- **A TWIST ON A POEM, SONG, BOOK, OR CLICHÉ:** *A Running Duck* by Paula Gosling; *A Is for Alibi* by Sue Grafton; *The Second Time Around* by Mary Higgins Clark; *There Was an Old Woman* by Hallie Ephron; *A Funny Thing Happened on the Way to the Future* by Michael J. Fox
- **THEME:** *Presumed Innocent* by Scott Turow; *The Blind Side* by Michael Lewis; *Grace (Eventually)* by Anne Lamott
- **SYMBOLISM:** *A Thief of Time* by Tony Hillerman; *Blink* by Malcolm Gladwell; *Light on Snow* by Anita Shreve
- **CHARACTER:** *Rebecca* by Daphne du Maurier; *Oprah* by Kitty Kelley; *Delores Claiborne* by Stephen King; *Saint Odd* by Dean Koontz

WORD COUNT: This is the number of words in your manuscript, which should correspond to the industry standard for your given subgenre.

TYPE OF BOOK: This is the genre or subgenre your work falls into: thriller, mystery, romance, memoir, self-help, how-to, graphic novel, etc.

UNIQUE SELLING PROPOSITION (USP): This is marketing-speak for what is unique about your book, what sets it apart from all the other books in its genre.

- **HIGH-CONCEPT PREMISE:** *Gone Girl* by Gillian Flynn; *Orphan Train* by Christina Baker Kline; *The Da Vinci Code* by Dan Brown
- **UNIQUE SETTING:** *The No. 1 Ladies' Detective Agency* by Alexander McCall Smith; *Eat, Pray, Love* by Elizabeth Gilbert; *The Martian* by Andy Weir
- **UNIQUE CHARACTERS:** *The Silence of the Lambs* by Thomas Harris; *In Cold Blood* by Truman Capote; *The Hunger Games* by Suzanne Collins
- **UNIQUE VOICE:** *My Horizontal Life* by Chelsea Handler; *Bird By Bird* by Anne Lamott; *Wild* by Cheryl Strayed
- **AUTHOR'S CREDENTIALS/HISTORY:** Joseph Wambaugh's cop novels; Margaret Truman's Capitol Crimes series; Chris Kyle's *American Sniper*; Rhoda Janzen's *Mennonite in a Little Black Dress*

Step Two: Briefly describe your credentials.

Your descriptions should pertain only to your ability to write this great book. Here are some examples:

- I'm a freelance writer who writes for *Great Desserts* magazine. That's why my memoir, *Chocoholic*, incorporates recipes, baking techniques, and quotes from famous pastry chefs and candy makers.
- I'm an attorney specializing in criminal law—so I made the protagonist in my legal thriller one, too.
- I do a lot of community theater, and I'm using my years as an actor to give *Summer Stock Murder* an authentic, insider tone.
- I'm a therapist who specializes in couples counseling in my private practice in Beverly Hills, and I draw upon that experience in my groundbreaking self-help book, *How to Stay Married Even When You're Rich and Famous.*

Step Three: *Expound on your description of your work and your credentials.*

If you're pitching in person, you need to be able to do this in lively and direct detail when asked. If you're writing a query letter, then you need do the same, but in writing. (See the samples later in this chapter.)

Step Four: *Prepare some questions.*

If you are pitching in person, think of a couple of questions you'd like to ask the agent or editor that might be pertinent to your project and the home it might find with this person. For example, you might ask her if she thinks your Southern setting is a selling point, or if she's had good experiences with independent publishers, or if your subgenre is selling well right now.

EVOLUTION OF AN ELEVATOR PITCH

Here's a pitch I helped a writer hone for his first pitching session at the New England Crime Bake. Let's take a look at each draft:

VERSION 1

> Tucker and his wife, Carol, worked together until the day he was fired and she was murdered. Now, haunted by Carol, he tries to find her killer in his old company. But office politics turn deadly as Tucker uncovers a conspiracy and a serial killer.

Comments: Good, but you should add something sexy about the setting—that is, the industry in which the story is set.

VERSION 2

> Tucker and his wife, Carol, worked together on spy software until the day he was fired and she was murdered. Now, haunted by Carol, he tries to find her killer in his

---

old company. But office politics turn deadly as Tucker uncovers a conspiracy and a serial killer.

Comments: Better, but still not specific enough. Fill in the blanks:

- _____ (alien, CIA, WHO, etc.) conspiracy
- _____ (saw-wielding, pyromaniac, schizophrenic, etc.) serial killer

---

VERSION 3

Über-geek Dan Tucker and his beautiful wife, Carol, developed top-secret spy software together until the day he was fired—and she was murdered. Haunted by his dead wife, Tucker is determined to track down her killer—no matter what the cost. Office politics turn deadly as Tucker takes on the FBI, Russian mobsters, and the serial killer known as the Duct Tape Strangler.

Comments: This is great, but you need to include the title, word count, and genre.

VERSION 4

In my 70,000-word thriller *Terminated,* über-geek Dan Tucker and his beautiful wife, Carol, develop top-secret spy software together, until the day he's fired—and she's murdered. Haunted by his dead wife, Tucker is determined to track down her killer—no matter what the cost. Office politics turn deadly as Tucker takes on the FBI, Russian mobsters, and the serial killer known as the Duct Tape Strangler.

Comments: Good to go!
I'm happy to say that Ray Daniel used this pitch to get an agent and a multibook deal. *Terminated* debuted to good reviews.

How to Write a Query

Now that you've developed your elevator pitch, you have the basis for a great query letter. Queries are the e-mails you send to agents and editors in the hope of interesting them in your work. Here's a template for a good query, part by part:

- **SUBJECT LINE:** This is the headline of your query.
- **SALUTATION:** "Dear X," X being the name of the intended recipient. Do spell X's name correctly, and never write "Dear Agent." If I had a dollar for every query that began "Dear Paul" or "Dear Agent" or "Dear Mr. Munier" …
- **PERSONAL TOUCH (OPTIONAL):** If you were referred by a mutual colleague or you met at a conference or whatever, refresh the agent's memory. Nicely.
- **ELEVATOR PITCH:** This is the pitch you've honed and honed and honed.
- **EXPANSION OF PITCH:** This is where you expand on your pitch, adding a plot point or two, a subplot, etc.
- **BIO:** This is a short (fifty-word) description of you, your credentials, and/or your platform, and how they inform your story.
- **CLOSING:** Say how much you'd like to send them a copy of your manuscript.
- **CONTACT INFO:** Your name, your e-mail, your phone number, your website, etc.

Here's a query I wrote for *Red Line*, the wonderful debut novel written by my swell client Brian Thiem. (You can pick up a copy of this great read wherever you like to buy your books.)

SAMPLE AGENT QUERY

[**Subject line**] Query: New Series by Oakland Homicide Detective

[**Salutation**] Hi Matt,

[**Personal touch**] I hope this finds you well and enjoying spring.

[**Elevator pitch**] I've got a great new project by a former Oakland homicide detective who can *actually* write. He's written a 90,000-word police procedural inspired by his thirty years in law enforcement. The first novel in his Matt Sinclair series is called *Red Line*:

Harry Bosch Meets Joseph Wambaugh

When someone starts murdering rich white people from other places and dumping them at an Oakland bus stop, homicide detective Matt Sinclair is assigned the case—his first since he was bumped to desk duty six months ago after a drug bust gone wrong. As the bodies pile up, Matt links the victims to a cold case he never solved. He's the reason people are dying—and if Matt doesn't find the killer in time, his lover Liz will be the next victim.

[**expansion of pitch**] *Red Line*—which refers to the line drawn through the case number when a murder is solved—is the compelling kind of police procedural that could only be written by a cop who's talked the talk and walked the walk and lived to tell about it.

[**Bio**] Brian Thiem spent twenty-five years with the Oakland Police Department, working Homicide as a detective sergeant and later as the commander of the Homicide Section, as well as patrol, special operations (SWAT), vice-narcotics, and in a variety of investigation and command positions before retiring as a Lieutenant. He also spent twenty-eight years of combined active and reserve duty in the Army, retiring as a Lieutenant Colonel, and serving in various Military Police and Criminal Investigation Division (CID) assignments, including a tour in Iraq as the Deputy Commander of the Criminal Investigation Group for the Middle East. He recently earned an MFA in Creative Writing from Western Connecticut State University.

[**Personal touch**] Brian is a great writer who's his own best advertisement. He wowed them at the recent New England Crime Bake, where he ran a class about how to write cops that sell.

[**Closing**] I'd love to send this to you for your review. I look forward to hearing from you.

[**Contact info**] Best,
Paula Munier
Talcott Notch Literary
www.talcottnotch.net
@PaulaSMunier

Of course, the queries you write to agents and editors will be written from a different point of view: yours. Here's a wonderful query I got from a writer that led to me signing her as a client and selling this story to a Big Five house in a very nice deal. (You can buy the compelling new adult novel *The Registry* by Shannon Stoker wherever you like to buy your books.)

SAMPLE WRITER QUERY

[**Subject line**] Query: The Registry

Paula Munier
Talcott Notch Literary Services, LLC
pmunier@talcottnotch.net

[**Salutation**] Dear Ms. Munier,

[**Elevator pitch**] *The Registry* is a 70,000-word, high-concept young adult novel aimed at thirteen- to eighteen-year-olds. In a world where all sixteen-year-old girls must enroll in the bridal registry, Mia Morrissey is willing to risk her life to avoid this fate.

[**Expansion of pitch**] Mia decides to run away from her arranged marriage. Since it is illegal for an unwed female to be out in public, she disguises herself as a boy and makes her way across the country. She forces seventeen-year-old Andrew to be her guide and help her avoid her madman fiancé, Grant, who is hot on their trail. As a relationship blooms between the two teenagers, another boy also catches Mia's eye. Now she has to focus on making her way to safety, avoiding Grant, and decoding her own romantic feelings.

[**Bio**] *The Registry* is my first novel. My previous writing experience includes fan fiction and legal blogs. I am currently a practicing attorney and decided it was time to write something fun.

[**Closing**] If you have any additional questions, please do not hesitate to contact me. I have included the first ten pages, as instructed by your website. Thank you for taking the time to consider my work.

[**Contact info**] Very truly yours,

Shannon R. Stoker
E-mail
Address
Phone number

Process and Persist

"You fail only if you stop writing." —RAY BRADBURY

You've written a great query, and you have a polished manuscript ready to send out. Now you need to come up with a list of agents (and editors) to query.

Any personal connection will help. As you've seen, agents (and editors) are swamped with queries and submissions. Speaking for myself—with the understanding that all agents and editors struggle with similar issues—my first responsibility is to my signed authors. My hands—and my in-box—are full with just the books I'm already working to sell. Of course, my secondary obligation is to find great new writers and projects—but that's something I mostly do after hours, in my so-called spare time. (Truth be told, almost all of my reading—and

I know that I am not alone in this—whether written by signed clients or potential clients, happens on evenings and weekends.)

The pile of projects waiting to be read is extremely high. At any given time, I have at least fifty projects to read in my secondary pile. (Yes, I'm a fast reader. No, I don't keep reading if the work is not well crafted.) Your goal is to get to the top of that secondary pile.

Anything that takes you out of the slush—the unsolicited work that comes dead last on the agent's to-do list—is a good thing. So if you can put "Referred by Editor X" or "Requested material from Conference Y" or "Pushcart Prize Nominee's New Novel" or "Forensics Expert's New Thriller" in the subject line of your e-mail query, you can set yourself apart in the in-box. When that's not an option, then make sure you have a heck of a headline.

Rejection Sucks. Get Over It.

"Rejection refines us. Those who fall prey to its enervating, soul-sucking tentacles are doomed. Those who persist past it are survivors. Best ask yourself the question: What kind of writer are you? The kind who survives? Or the kind who gets asphyxiated by the tentacles of woe?" —CHUCK WENDIG

Once you start sending out queries, the waiting begins. The wait can be interminable—first to hear back from the agents and then to hear back from the editors your agent contacts to read your work. I tell people to "pester me nicely" every week until I read their work, and I'll be the first to admit that it can take a long time for me to read it.

That's why you never send your work to just one agent at a time. Feel free to submit to multiple parties. If an agent asks for an exclusive, meaning that you offer her alone the opportunity to read your work for a limited period of time, you can grant it—but for no more than two weeks.

You'll probably collect more than one rejection on your path to publication. But that's the nature of the business. Don't let this get you down or deter you in any way. If you receive any specific feedback (as opposed to a generic rejection letter), then you should congratulate yourself—and listen to that feedback. If someone asks you to revise and resubmit, then do it. (I've signed more than one client after the writer revised the work based on my feedback.)

Whatever you do, don't be rude, snarky, or a pain in the butt. Don't trash people, at least not publicly, online or elsewhere. Publishing is a small world, and the rules of business etiquette apply here, too. Be polite and professional, no matter what.

And keep on submitting your work. While you wait, write the next book.

"Every rejection is incremental payment on your dues that in some way will be translated back into your work." —James Lee Burke

THE "BUSINESS" OF PUBLISHING

When an agent offers to represent you, have a frank and open conversation to help you figure out if this agent is right for you. Here are some areas you might want to cover:

- **COMMISSION STRUCTURE.** The standard is 15 percent of sales, with 20 percent for foreign and film. No agent should charge reading fees.
- **THE SCOPE OF REVISIONS, IF NEEDED.**
- **A SUBMISSION PLAN.** Like many agents, I prepare a submission plan to share with each client.
- **THE PREFERRED MEANS OF COMMUNICATION.** E-mail, phone, text, etc. I tell my clients to text me; I also have a separate e-mail for clients and editors only.
- **TRANSPARENCY.** This can vary according to the preferences of the agent and the client. I report all feedback to my clients—unless

they are too thin-skinned to hear it. Which is not a good thing, in my humble opinion.

- **CAREER.** Make sure you are both on the same page in terms of where you want to go in your career and how you want to get there.

The most important thing may be the agent's enthusiasm for your work. You want an agent who believes in you and your work, and who shares a similar vision for your career.

The Good News Is You've Got an Agent

When you do sign with an agent, you are entering a professional relationship. Your agent is not your secretary or your shrink or your mother; your agent is your publishing advocate. It's a partnership, dedicated to furthering your publishing career. Remember that your agent doesn't get paid until he sells your work, so the fact that he believes in you and your work strongly enough to take you on for a commission that may or may not happen already indicates a commitment on his part. With any luck, this relationship will prove one of the most stimulating, long-lasting, beneficial, and profitable associations of your professional life. Like a good marriage, you should remember to enjoy and appreciate it.

That said, not every agent-author relationship works out that way. If your agent fails to sell your work, don't automatically assume that it's her fault. Ask to see the feedback she's received—and take it seriously. Sometimes it's the revised version of the book that sells, the one you fixed after an early round of submission based on feedback from editors. Or sometimes, it's the next book that sells.

Sometimes your partnership runs its course, or turns out not to be a good fit, and you should move on. But do discuss any issues you may have with your agent; I'm always surprised at the many writers I meet who have complained publicly and privately about their agents to anyone who will listen but have never actually voiced their complaints to the agents themselves. That's like getting a divorce without ever telling your spouse why you're leaving. Talk to your agent, and maybe you can work it out. If not, you can leave with no regrets.

THE BUSINESS OF PROMOTION

The business of publishing has changed more in the past twenty years—and especially in the past five years—than it has since Gutenberg invented the printing press back in the fifteenth century. The rise and decline of the chain bookstores, the e-book revolution, the proliferation of online publishers and booksellers, the predominance of social media—all these factors and more have changed the book business in profound ways that we haven't even begun to understand yet. And that change will continue.

All this change affects the way you do business as a writer. Once you find a publisher, you can't just sit back and rest on your contract. In the old days, authors were reliant upon their publishers to promote and market their work—and if you were a small fish in a big pond, your books often got overlooked, as publishers reserved the bulk of their publicity and marketing budgets for the brand-name authors.

But authors no longer have to rely on the publisher; the good news is that the digital world we now live in offers you the opportunity to drive your own PR and marketing. You can generate great PR, build your readership, and boost your sales on your own and/or in coordination with your publisher's efforts. You need to show your publisher and your readers that you are committed to promoting and selling your books.

You can begin building your platform before you even write a word. But once the contract is signed and you know that you have a book coming out, you certainly need to focus on this. These are the strategies I advise my clients to consider:

1. Hire a blog tour manager to set up blog tours for you to promote your book.
2. Ramp up your social media efforts. This means a website and a Facebook page, of course, but also a marketing campaign that includes:

   - contests
   - giveaways

- blogs
- newsletters
- Skyping with book clubs
- writing short pieces for online publications popular with your readership
- hanging out on Facebook, Twitter, Pinterest, Instagram, and wherever your readership hangs out online

3. Find your readers and court them. If you can afford it, it's also worth investing in a publicist who's savvy about social media and can help you create a social media campaign. Ask for recommendations from your editor, your agent, or successful authors in your genre.
4. Check out other successful authors in your genre and do whatever they are doing. Study their strategies and adopt them.
5. Ask your friends and fans to write reviews on Goodreads and Amazon. Return the favor.
6. Join SCBWI, RWA, SFWA, MWA, Sisters in Crime, and so on. Go to meetings and conferences; volunteer. Work with other published authors in your genre to do group blogs, group signings, and group appearances, both online and off-line. These groups typically afford you the opportunity to:

   - set up your books for sale in the bookstore.
   - register yourself in the speakers' bureau.
   - access members-only resources including directories, podcasts, and newsletter archives.
   - check out and register for events anywhere in the world.
   - set up a membership profile.
   - become a part of the organization's discussion boards, forum, and online chapters.
   - get recommendations for blogs to read.

7. If there's any romance in your story at all, check out *Romantic Times* (which is where many independent booksellers look for titles; the independents are growing in number now in the wake of

the chains' decline). Consider advertising your book in *Romantic Times*. (The lead time can be as long as six months, so arrange this accordingly.) Also of interest in RT: www.rtbookreviews.com. This section is available online and goes out to a huge readership.

8. Start getting yourself invited to conferences, where you can do the following things:

   - sign books.
   - appear on panels.
   - meet fans, reviewers, and booksellers.

9. Read books on promotion and marketing:

   - *Your First 1000 Copies* by Tim Grahl
   - *Create Your Writer Platform* by Chuck Sambuchino
   - *Sell Your Book Like Wildfire* by Rob Eagar
   - *Social Media Just for Writers* by Frances Caballo
   - *Platform* by Michael Hyatt

DRILL IT DOWN

Do a survey of the websites, Facebook pages, and social media campaigns of several successful authors in your genre. Which of these strategies might you adopt to help build your platform and PR and marketing efforts?

THE RISE AND FALL AND RISE (AGAIN) OF NEWSLETTERS

In the middle of writing this chapter, I participated in a conference call with one of my clients and the marketing and publicity people assigned to his book by his Big Five publisher. They were very hot on e-mail newsletters, saying that authors with newsletters have a direct line to their readership. This allows authors to offer their newsletter subscribers special giveaways, excerpts, news, and more. *Note:* Newsletters were popular for a while, then lost ground to blogs, but now apparently are back on top. This just goes to show how quickly things change in the electronic world and how it's up to you to keep up with those changes—so you can keep up with your readership.

This is important: Now is the time to *invest in your success and build your readership,* so that you can sell your new book when the time comes. You need to do all you can to help your book find its place in the market, because you'll be judged by its sales forever. You don't want to be one of those writers who have to change their names and their genres to get a second book published after the first failed. This happens too often, so be sure to do your part to promote and market your book.

Because a writer with an audience is a writer with a career.

HANDS ON

Make a list of the ways in which you can grow your platform now. If your personal or professional life informs your work, brainstorm how you might use that expertise and/or experience to start building an audience.

"I talk to my readers on social networking sites, but I never tell them what the book is about. Writing is lonely, so from time to time I talk to them on the Internet. It's like chatting at a bar without leaving your office. I talk with them about a lot of things other than my books." —PAULO COELHO

CHAPTER SIXTEEN

wherever you write, there you are

"So what will you do today, knowing that you are one of the rarest forms of life to ever walk the earth? How will you carry yourself? What will you do with your hands?" —MARK NEPO

As I begin to write this last chapter, snow is falling, falling, falling. I look out my living room at the lake behind the cottage, where the record snowfall has drifted in high swells across its wide frozen face. It's been snowing ceaselessly for two weeks now, and much of Boston is literally snowbound. The trains aren't running and the roads aren't plowed and the weatherman says that more snow is on the way.

Even the hardiest New Englanders are growing cranky. Spring is still an endless thirty-nine days away. Nobody can go anywhere—and the few people who try are mostly stuck cursing in their cars on the highway. Cabin fever is setting in; a collective cloud of discontent has descended upon the Commonwealth.

I can't go anywhere, either, but I don't care. I have heat and power and the blank page before me. While the rest of my compatriots shovel on, planning trips to Florida and preparing to list their homes for sale and move south come spring, I'm on holiday—an unexpected writer's retreat, courtesy of Mother Nature. I couldn't be happier.

This is the glory of being a writer. This is the reward of writing with quiet hands. Faced with enforced solitude, we are content to sit tight and write on.

A QUESTION OF CRAFT

Often the gift of unexpected writing time comes disguised as an inconvenience—bad weather, cancelled plans, a long wait at the DMV. When you are blessed with such a gift, do you see it as a blessing? Do you take advantage of it? Do you sit tight and write on?

(REMEMBER) WHY YOU WRITE

"Writing is the only thing that when I do it, I don't feel I should be doing something else."
—GLORIA STEINEM

Often the accoutrements of the writing life—the effort to get published, dealing with agents and editors and publishers and booksellers and readers, the obligatory promotion and marketing activities, the pressure to sell, sell, sell books—can interfere with the writing process. To paraphrase E.L. Doctorow, anything that happens to a writer can be bad—failure and success, fame and fortune, obscurity and poverty, praise and pans.

The literary landscape is littered with writers who give up too soon. One of my most-talented clients stopped writing, depressed because her first novel did not sell. I told her to write the next novel and let this one go. This is what I tell all of my clients, but I can't make them listen. The ones who go on and write the next novel—and the next and the next—get published. Most writers do not sell their first novel. But they sell their second or third or fourth one. They keep writing because they are writers. They don't let failure stop them; they keep writing with quiet hands.

Once you start putting your work out there, it takes on a life of its own—and you have no control over it. The more you worry about it, or try to manipulate its future, the more miserable you become. And the less new writing you do. Putting your story into the world is like realizing that your children are all grown up and ready to leave home. They need to fly solo. They no longer belong to you. If you've done your job right, they know that—and they are free to embark, unfettered, in search of their destiny. And you need to let them go. Otherwise you may never hear from them again—or when you do, it's against their will. They'll come back to you when they are good and ready, on their own terms.

The same is true for your work. It no longer belongs to you. It belongs to the readers, however many or few they may be. Just as you may applaud your adult children's triumphs or bemoan their setbacks, you may applaud and bemoan your work. But you can't fuss over every bump in the road. And there will be bumps.

Victory can be just as debilitating as defeat. Think of Margaret Mitchell, who was so disconcerted by the overwhelming success of *Gone with the Wind* that she never wrote another book. Or Harper Lee, who is finally publishing another book after her monumental achievement, *To Kill a Mockingbird,* silenced her for decades. But this book, *Go Set a Watchman*, is one she wrote *before* she wrote the novel that made—and destroyed—her as a writer.

No matter what happens to your stories once they enter the universe of readers, remember why you write. Hold on to your muse. Persist in your writing practice. Continue to master your craft, and take pride and pleasure in your craftsmanship.

Ultimately all that matters is your relationship to your writing self. Do whatever you have to do to keep that relationship happy, healthy, and productive.

Because you're in this for the long haul.

"For me, writing a novel is like having a dream. Writing a novel lets me intentionally dream while I'm still awake. I can continue yesterday's dream today, something you can't normally do in everyday life." —HARUKI MURAKAMI

WRITERS WITH QUIET HANDS

When you need a little inspiration or the muse is eluding you or you're in danger of forgetting why you write, here are the works that can help you remember:

- *Bird by Bird* by Anne Lamott
- *On Writing* by Stephen King
- *The Book of Awakening* by Mark Nepo
- *Writing Down the Bones* by Natalie Goldberg
- *Walden* by Henry David Thoreau
- *One Writer's Beginnings* by Eudora Welty
- *New and Selected Poems, Volume Two* by Mary Oliver
- *Zen in the Art of Writing* by Ray Bradbury
- *The Artist's Way* by Julia Cameron
- *The Writing Life* by Annie Dillard
- *The Paris Review* series
- *The New Yorker* writer interviews
- *Charlie Rose* show writer interviews

"People spend a lifetime thinking about how they would really like to live. I asked my friends, and no one seems to know very clearly. To me it's very clear now. I wish my life could have been like the years when I was writing *Love in the Time of Cholera*." —GABRIEL GARCÍA MÁRQUEZ

WRITE IT DOWN

Get a pen and some paper, and set the timer for twenty minutes. Write about what success as a writer means to you. Dream big for your story—and detail which destiny you'd choose for it, if you could. When you are finished, fold up that paper and slip it into the back of your sock drawer—and forget about it.

THE LONG HAUL

"I am large, I contain multitudes." —WALT WHITMAN

When you write with quiet hands, you have the tools you need to be in this writing game for the long haul. Approaching your writing as a craftsperson gives you permission to play. To go big.

Part of surviving and thriving over a lifetime of writing is allowing yourself to grow, to push your own limits, to reach for the stars in your own creator's universe.

Or, as I like to tell my clients and writing students: Write epic shit.

Go for broke with every book. Tell the story you thought you couldn't tell—and trust that you'll develop the craftsmanship you need to tackle that too-big story as you write it. Because you will.

Trust the writing process itself—and you will prosper. Don't worry about the critics. Don't let the naysayers win. There'll always be plenty of people around to tell you that you suck, that your writing sucks, that there's not a snowball's chance in hell that you'll ever make it as a writer. Ignore them. Most of the time they are motivated by jealousy or cynicism or mean-spiritedness that has nothing to do with you. (My mother would give me this advice when I was a little girl and one of my peers hurt my feelings. I never believed her. Then I grew up and became a writer and realized that in this, as in many other things, she was right.)

Once you get published, this criticism will only increase. In fact, they'll actually *pay* people to put you and your work down. (They're called critics.) You'll need to learn to process any constructive criticism you may receive and delete the rest from your memory banks forever.

I learned this early on in my career, when I was the editor of a business publication in Monterey. I'd written an innocuous profile of a local business, the sort of predictable feature one finds in such weekly newspapers. And yet this story, humble as it was, enraged two readers enough to prompt them to write angry Letters to the Editor. One called me a fascist; the other called me a communist. Both called for my dismissal.

Luckily my publisher believed that if you didn't provoke at least one reader to write an irate Letter to the Editor every week, you weren't doing your job. He was inordinately pleased with me. I was relieved—and from that moment forward paid very little attention to most of my critics.

"I cannot greatly care what critics say of my work; if it is good, it will come to the surface in a generation or two and float, and if not, it will sink, having in the meantime provided me with a living, the opportunities of leisure, and a craftsman's intimate satisfactions." —JOHN UPDIKE

Ignoring such attacks can prove difficult. Fail to do so, however, and the barbs can fester, poisoning your will to write and/or publish your work. Sometimes it helps to ritualize the process of letting criticism go. A couple of years after I received those accusatory Letters to the Editor, I was serving as the editor of Santa Cruz County's alternative weekly newspaper, *Good Times*. One of my reporters wrote a story that infuriated a reader, who wrote a long, vicious diatribe denouncing the story and its writer. Our policy was to print every Letter to the Editor, whether flattering or unflattering. Everyone on the editorial staff had read the letter. The reporter was embarrassed and humiliated.

I could tell that she was taking the letter's unfounded accusations and criticisms too much to heart. So I had her make a copy of the original letter. I invited my entire editorial staff, all of whom were upset about the incident, out to the parking lot behind our offices.

"Time for a ritual burning." I gathered the group into a circle and held up the offensive missive. "We all know that this is crap written by a crank. Let's give it the reception it deserves."

Everyone laughed, a little nervously, as no one was quite sure if I was joking or not.

I borrowed a cigarette lighter from one of the smokers in the crowd and handed it, along with the copy of the letter, to the reporter. "Why don't you do the honors?"

The reporter grinned and set the letter afire. Everyone cheered.

With the criticism literally up in smoke, the reporter continued to write great stories, for that publication as well as many others. Now she's a published author and, I'm happy to say, my client. As I write this, I'm getting ready to shop her first novel.

Whenever your critics put you down, conduct your own ritual burning. If that's a little too harsh for you, then do what we do in yoga—and release your critics to their own destinies. Karma, baby—it's what all unreasonable and unjust critics deserve.

"If you wrote something for which someone sent you a check, if you cashed the check and it didn't bounce, and if you then paid the light bill with the money, I consider you talented." —STEPHEN KING

DRILL IT DOWN

According to a study in the *Review of General Psychology*, people remember criticism far longer than praise. What's the worst criticism you've received as a writer? Was there anything you could learn from it? Does it still haunt you? Write down the worst things anyone's ever said to you about your writing. Now perform a ritual burning of your own.

YOU ON A BOOK COVER

"Writing isn't about making money, getting famous, getting dates, getting laid, or making friends. In the end, it's about enriching the lives of those who will read your work, and enriching your own life, as well. It's about getting up, getting well, and getting over. Getting happy, okay? Getting happy."
—STEPHEN KING

We all dream about getting published. We all picture our stories on the bestseller lists. We all long to be the ones who follow in the footsteps of the great storytellers we love and admire.

How many times have we heard of some churlish action on the part of a rich and famous writer and shaken our heads in dismay: Jonathan Franzen insulting the readers of Oprah's Book Club, James Frey making up parts of his memoir, Norman Mailer stabbing his wife.

If we were ever lucky enough to be those guys, well, we wouldn't be *those guys.*

If we were ever lucky enough to be published, we'd be generous and magnanimous to family and friends and fans alike. We'd be as enthusiastic about our craft and as encouraging to new writers as Ray Bradbury was. We'd give away as much money to good causes as Nora Roberts and Isabel Allende and J.K. Rowling and Jonathan Keller-man and Dean Koontz do. We'd keep stretching our limits and writing through thick and thin, like Joyce Carol Oates and Isaac Asimov. In short, we'd be *swell.*

Well, now's the time to prove it. The time to be that writer, the one you promised you would be before you got published. Gracious. Graceful. Grateful.

Writing is nothing less than a path to enlightenment. The best writers are the writers whose work is enlightened by experience and polished by craftsmanship. These are the writers who write with quiet hands.

Just like you.

HANDS ON

What's the too-big story you think you aren't able to write? Begin it.

"Because this business of becoming conscious, of being a writer, is ultimately about asking yourself, 'How alive am I willing to be?'" —ANNE LAMOTT

acknowledgments

This was a book dear to my heart—and I thank Phil Sexton, publisher of Writer's Digest and all-around good guy, for paying me to write it. And to all my friends at Writer's Digest, including my wonderful editor, Rachel Randall; Cris Freese; Alex Rixey; Chuck Sambuchino; Kevin Quinn; Aaron Bauer; Sue Johnson; and Kimberly Catanzarite.

I must also thank my sister agents at Talcott Notch Literary, including Rachael Dugas, Saba Sulaiman, and our fearless leader, Gina Panettieri. And my folks, Paul and Marilyn Munier, who appear in virtually everything I write, in one way or another, whether they like it or not.

And a shout-out to the wonderful authors whose commitment to craft inspires me every day, including Hank Phillippi Ryan, Hallie Ephron, William Martin, Joseph Finder, Julia Spencer-Fleming, Craig Johnson, Tess Gerritsen, Trish MacGregor, Rob MacGregor, Julia Cameron, Lee Child, Reed Farrel Coleman, Harlen Coben, Jane Cleland, Alice Hoffman, Claire Cook, Mark Nepo, Mary Oliver, Anne Lamott, Elizabeth Berg, and so many more. Thank you especially to the colleagues and clients whose stories brighten this book and my writing life, including Rob Brancatelli, John K. Waters, Indi Zeleny, Shannon Stoker, Brian Thiem, Kim Van Alkemade, Michele Dorsey, J.J. Partridge, Larry Kay, Jess Anastasi, Cate Holahan, Cynthia Riggs, Meera Lester, Susan Reynolds, Mardeene Mitchell, Margaret McLean, Rich Krevolin, Brian Thornton, Greg Bergman, Alexis Munier, Michael Lee, Richard Thomas, Kate Defrise, Jim Shannon, Dick Cass, Tom Owens, Vaughn Hardacker, Gail Greiner, Ethan Ellenberg, Jon Kennedy, Ray Daniel, Kate Flora, Steve Ulfelder, and everyone on the New England Crime Bake Committee.

And a final heartfelt thanks to all of the writers who've shared their time and work with me over the years, and to you, my readers.

May you write with quiet hands, always.

about the author

Paula Munier, senior literary agent and content strategist at Talcott Notch Literary Services, boasts broad experience creating and marketing exceptional content in all formats across all markets for such media giants as WGBH, Disney, Fidelity, Gannett, Greenspun Media Group, F+W Media, and Quayside. She began her career as a journalist and along the way added editor, acquisitions specialist, digital-content manager, and publishing executive to her repertoire. Her specialties include literary fiction, women's fiction, historical fiction, mystery/thriller, SF/fantasy, romance, YA, memoir, humor, pop culture, health and wellness, cooking, self-help, pop psych, New Age, inspirational, technology, science, and writing. Paula is very involved with the mystery community, having served four terms as president of the New England chapter of Mystery Writers of America as well as on the MWA board.

Paula has also served on the New England Crime Bake committee for ten years and counting, and she's an active member of Sisters in Crime and SCBWI. A well-published journalist, author, copywriter, and ghostwriter, Paula has penned countless news stories, articles, essays, collateral, and blogs, as well as authored/co-authored more than a dozen books, including *Plot Perfect*, *Fixing Freddie*, and *5-Minute Mindfulness*.

index